The Flags of the Iron Brigade

The Flags
of the
Iron Brigade

By Howard Michael Madaus and Richard H. Zeitlin

Wisconsin Veterans Museum

1997

Published by the Wisconsin Veterans Museum
30 West Mifflin Street
Madison, WI 53703

ISBN: 0–9655854–0–9

Acknowledgments

A number of people and organizations have contributed to this publication. I want to recognize the help of Paul Hass of the State Historical Society of Wisconsin for his sound advice, his generosity of spirit, and interest in the subject. Lance Herdegen of the Caroll College Civil War Institute also encouraged the production efforts while providing suggestions and good cheer. The G.A.R. Memorial Association of Dane County, Inc. donated generously to the printing effort, and the long term support of Thomas L. W. Johnson has been appreciated. Robert Needham provided the line drawings. Recognizing Needham's work for its accuracy and quality is a pleasure.

The Wisconsin Department of Veterans Affairs, which operates the Wisconsin Veterans Museum, is a constant source of strength and support. Agency Secretary Raymond Boland, along with his able executive team Robert Cocroft and Charles Hoslet, have been allies and partners in my work. Karen Gulbrandsen, Curator of Programs at the Veterans Museum, is one of the most able editors I have encountered. For her efficient, sensitive, and thoughtful suggestions concerning production matters, I wholeheartedly acknowledge a debt of gratitude. The support of the Institute of Museum Studies is likewise acknowledged. Errors in judgment and presentation remain my own.

Richard H. Zeitlin

Prefatory Note

Nearly 3 million men served in the Union Army during the Civil War, 1861–1865. Of these, some 5,000 men filled the ranks of the Iron Brigade, which was made up of the Second, Sixth, and Seventh Wisconsin, the Nineteenth Indiana, and the Twenty-Fourth Michigan Volunteer Infantry regiments. As the only "all Western" unit in President Abraham Lincoln's Army of the Potomac, the Iron Brigade compiled an unsurpassed record of bravery and sacrifice. No brigade in the Union Army suffered a higher percentage of combat fatalities, and the Second Wisconsin sustained the highest percentage of fatal casualties among the 3,559 Union regiments in the war. The training, leadership, and morale of the officers and men of the Iron Brigade were conspicuous at Gainesville, South Mountain, Antietam, Gettysburg, and a dozen other battles and skirmishes. "At such places, and on more than one occasion," recalled one of their commanders, "brave men died to keep their flags aloft." Always the flags were in the forefront of battle, proudly displayed, tenaciously defended. In a day when soldiers entered battle to the sounds of fife and drum, the regimental colors came to represent, as few tangible objects could, the very ideal of the Union. How the flags of the Iron Brigade came to be, and what purposes they served both during and after the war, is the topic of this two-part publication.

Part I

Into the Fray

Into the Fray:
The Flags of the Iron Brigade, 1863–1918

By Howard Michael Madaus

. . . We moved on to battle, and soon the whole ground shook at the discharges of artillery and infantry. Gainesville, Bull Run, South Mountain were good respectable battles, but in the intensity and energy of the fight and the roar of the firearms, they were but skirmishes in comparison to this of Sharpsburg. . . . About twenty stands of colors were captured by us,—two by the 6th Wisc. The flag of the 6th received four bullets in the flag staff, and some fifteen in the fly,—that of the 2nd Wisc. three bullets in the staff and more than twenty in the fly. We are now near the field. I hope you may never have occasion to see such a sight as it is.[1]

Lieutenant Frank A. Haskell of Portage, the author of this passage, is better known for his firsthand account of the battle of Gettysburg. He saw action on some of the bloodiest battlefields of the Civil War, and he was not given to exaggeration. When he posted this description of the battle of Antietam (or Sharpsburg) to his brothers and sisters during the autumn of 1862, he had been serving for four months on the staff of Brigadier General John Gibbon. The shot-torn flags Haskell made note of—those of the Sixth Wisconsin and the Second Wisconsin—represented two of the regiments comprising Gibbon's Brigade, a unit that had won the nickname "Iron Brigade" for its action at South Mountain, just three days before the appalling slaughter at Antietam. In succeeding months—at Fredericksburg, Chancellorsville, and above all on the first day at Gettysburg—

---

[1]Lieutenant Frank A. Haskell, letter of September 22, 1862, originally published October 4, 1862, in the Portage *Wisconsin State Register.* See E.B. Quiner, "Correspondence of Wisconsin Volunteers, 1861–1865," Vol. 4, pp. 18–19, unprocessed papers, 1861–1865, Wisconsin State Archives, State Historical Society of Wisconsin; hereinafter cited as CWV. See also Frank L. Byrne and Andrew T. Weaver, eds., *Haskell of Gettysburg: His Life and Civil War Papers* (Madison, 1970), 47–48.

the midwesterners of Gibbon's Brigade amply justified their claim to being the bravest of the brave among all the regiments of the Union Army.

The story of the Iron Brigade's march to glory has been told elsewhere.[2] Nevertheless, one aspect of the brigade's history remains virtually untold: the story of the brigade's flags. These now decayed remnants of silk tell a special tale of America's most destructive conflict.

During the American Civil War, as in earlier conflicts, the flags of a combat unit (its "colors") held a special significance. They had a spiritual value; they embodied the very "soul" of the unit. W.H. Druen of Rockville, Wisconsin, witnessed the attachment the men had to their colors when he wrote home on August 1, 1861:[3]

> We are the color company of the Sixth Regiment, and carry the regimental colors; and I feel safe in saying in behalf of Company 'C' that the splendid flag entrusted to our care, shall not be dishonored by any act of ours. We shall bring it back unsullied by traitors' hands.

Indeed, the loss of its colors in combat could seriously jeopardize the morale of that unit. After the regimental color of the Sixth Wisconsin briefly fell into the hands of the Eightieth New York at the battle of Antietam, Lieutenant Colonel Edward S. Bragg felt it necessary to explain[4]

> . . . that the regiment conducted itself during the fight so as to fully sustain its previous reputation; that it did not abandon its colors on the field; that every color-bearer and every member of the guard was disabled and compelled to leave; that the State color fell into other keeping, temporarily, in rear of the regiment, because its bearer had fallen; but it was immediately reclaimed, and under its folds, few but undaunted,

---

[2]Alan T. Nolan, *The Iron Brigade: A Military History* (2nd ed., Madison, 1975). No fewer than five regimental histories have been published about the regiments of the brigade and numerous articles.

[3]CWV, Vol. 1, pp. 238–240.

[4]U.S. War Department, *The War of the Rebellion: A Compilation of the Official Records of the Union and Confederate Armies* (Washington, 1880–1901), Series I, Vol. 19, Pt. 1, p. 255; hereinafter cited as *OR*. See p. 247 of the same volume for the report that instigated Bragg's remarks.

the regiment rallied to the support of the battery. The
color lance of the National color is pierced with five
balls, and both colors bear multitudes of testimony
that they were in the thickest of the fight.

But beyond these transcendental factors, flags served at least
three practical purposes on the nineteenth century battlefield.

A t the beginning of the Civil War, colorful uniforms were
adopted or adapted from pre-war militia service by the
belligerents of both sides to enhance unit morale or state pride.
Such uniforms were not always conducive to distinguishing friend
from foe. Indeed, the Second Wisconsin, outfitted by Wisconsin
in gray uniforms, found itself under fire from both friend and
foe during the first battle of Bull Run! The thick gray-white smoke
that clung near the ground on battlefields of the black-powder
era further complicated the problem. In such circumstances, flags
were often the only means of distinguishing the identity of the
combatants.

Unit flags also served as the focal point for maintaining alignment within the unit during an era when linear tactics predomi-
nated. The single-shot, muzzle-loading musket dictated that
infantry fight in closely formed, standing lines of battle to achieve
effective concentration of fire. In spite of the revolution caused
by the adoption of the rifle-musket, which increased the effective range of a regiment from seventy-five yards to well over
250 yards, the battles of 1861 and early 1862 were largely fought
with the smoothbore muskets of earlier periods, and officers
were trained to handle their men accordingly. Volley fire (ne-
cessitated by the inherent inaccuracy of the smoothbore musket) demanded strict attention to proper alignment of all segments
of a military unit, lest a portion of the unit's fire fall harmlessly
short. The unit's colors, situated in the center of the firing line,
provided the focal point by which company commanders aligned
their formations within the unit before firing. "Guiding upon the
colors" remained an important command even after the rifle-musket drastically altered the necessity for strict lineal alignment.

Lastly, flags served as the focus for leading an assault or for
rallying a broken unit. Where the colors went, the men followed. Describing his part at Antietam after he had recovered

the unit's state flag, Major Rufus R. Dawes of the Sixth Wisconsin recollected:[5]

> At the bottom of the hill I took the blue color of the State of Wisconsin, and waving it, called a rally of Wisconsin men. Two hundred men gathered around the flag of the Badger state. . . . I commanded 'Right face, forward march,' and started ahead with the colors in my hand into the open field, the men following.

And, where the colors went, men usually died.

Because the colors drew an inordinate share of enemy fire and were the object of capture, the color-party of the period was large and more than ceremonial. The national color was carried by a sergeant, while the regimental or state color was carried by a corporal. Anywhere from four to seven other corporals were selected to form the color-guard,[6] whose sole duty in combat consisted of protecting the unit's flags. Only after the flag was removed from a functional combat role did military tacticians reduce the size of the color-guard.

The importance of flags to military units during the mid-nineteenth century was not limited to the military tacticians who prepared the drill manuals that officers studied for the rudiments of marching and maneuvers. Patriotic groups and individuals throughout the country answered Lincoln's initial call to arms by presenting flags to the militia and volunteer companies that answered. Loyal Wisconsinites were no different than their compatriots throughout the North.

---

[5]Rufus R. Dawes, *Service with the Sixth Wisconsin Volunteers* (Marietta, Ohio, 1890), 91.

[6]U.S. War Department, *U.S. Infantry Tactics, for the Instruction, Exercise, and Manoeuvres of the United States Infantry, Including Infantry of the Line, Light Infantry, and Riflemen. . .* (Philadelphia, 1861), 10–11. Originally translated from the French in 1855 by then Major William J. Hardee, this same plan of organizing the nine-man color-party was incorporated into the tactical manuals of Silas Casey (1862), Henry Coppee (1862), William Gilham (1861), the Confederate edition of William J. Hardee (1861), and H.B. Wilson (1862). The six-man or optional nine-man color-party had been regulation from 1835 through 1855 when supplanted by Hardee's tactics. Nevertheless, the outdated *Infantry Tactics, or Rules for the Exercise and Manoeuvres of the United States Infantry* was reprinted in New York in both 1858 and 1861 under the deceptive guise of being a "new edition," and was extensively used. Similarly, Captain S. Cooper's 1836 synopsis of this older tactical system was reprinted under Captain M. Knowleton's deceptively titled *Authorized Tactics, U.S.A.*, including Cooper's paragraph on the six-man color-party, verbatim.

Wisconsin's quota under Lincoln's initial call was for but a single infantry regiment of ten companies. Ten pre-war militia companies quickly volunteered their services for three months' service, filled their ranks with recruits, and gathered at the old fair grounds in Milwaukee to be equipped by the state. One item the state did not provide the First Wisconsin Active Militia was a flag. The nimble fingers of the patriotic ladies of Milwaukee quickly fashioned silk into a fine national flag decorated with thirty-four silver stars, and on May 8, 1861, Governor Alexander Randall traveled to Milwaukee to officially present the flag to the regiment on behalf of the ladies. The Horicon Guards, Company C of the First Wisconsin, also received an elegant silk national flag bearing a painted American eagle in its canton, a gift of the ladies of Horicon.[7] Like most of the company flags presented to departing local units in 1861, that of the Horicon Guards never saw combat.

The enthusiasm that led to the formation of the First Wisconsin Active Militia brought offers for service from far more companies than there were positions available. Although Washington did not authorize it, Governor Randall organized the overflow into a second regiment of "State Active Militia" for three months' service and established its rendezvous at Madison. The militia companies volunteering for this Second Regiment soon flocked to Camp Randall, many encumbered with flags that had been presented by the communities whence they had departed.

The La Crosse Light Guards (Company B of the Second Regiment) arrived with a "white silk flag, with blue fringe and inscribed on an oval ground in the centre: 'Presented by the ladies of La Crosse, July 4th 1860, to the La Crosse Light Guards.'" The Portage Light Guards (Company G) arrived with a silk national

Presentation color of the Miners Guard, Company I, Second Wisconsin Infantry, 1861.

[7]The *Milwaukee Sentinel*, May 8 and 9, 1861. For the account of the Horicon Guard's flag, see CWV, Vol. 1, p. 3, clipping dated May 5, 1861.
[8]CWV, Vol.1, p. 70.

flag presented by the ladies of the city prior to the company's departure. Both companies arrived in the predominately gray uniforms adopted prior to hostilities.[8] The Janesville Volunteers (Company D) arrived without uniforms, but boasted "a superb national flag of silk" carried by Ensign Dana D. Dodge.[9] Similarly, the Miners Guard (Company I) arrived only partly uniformed. Nevertheless, the ladies of Mineral Point had completed a "handsome merino United States flag" presented by G.W. Cobb before the company departed on its stormy ride to Madison in open wagons.[10]

The most impressive flag, however, was that brought to Camp Randall by the Belle City Rifles (Company F). The young ladies of Racine had presented a color to this company in impressive ceremonies at Titus Hall prior to its departure. The local newspapers described it in some detail:[11]

> It is of dark blue silk, with a silver fringe. On one side is painted a shield inscribed 'Racine, 1861' with a national flag draped on either side of it, surmounted by an eagle holding the bolts of Jove. Over is the motto 'Remember Sumter,' and on scrolls near the centre, 'For Freedom,' and 'For God.' On the reverse is a shield with a star, surrounded by military emblems, with the name of the company inscribed.

The flag was attached to a staff bearing a spearpoint and adorned with a set of "heavy cord and tassels."

Once the regiment had assembled at Camp Randall, there was little use for these patriotic company gifts. In the absence of regimental colors, the colonel may have occasionally selected one or two of the company colors to accompany regimental drill, and they undoubtedly decorated the tents of the respective captains. The drill manuals and the *Army Regulations*, however, permitted only one set of colors per regiment, and the company flags were accordingly relegated to the captains' baggage.

---

[9] *Ibid.*, Vol. 1, p. 72.
[10] *Ibid.*, Vol. 1, p. 72.
[11] *Ibid.*, Vol. 1, p. 72; *cf* also p. 125.

The *Revised United States Army Regulations of 1861* ordained that each infantry regiment was to have a set of colors consisting of two flags. Each was supposed to measure seventy-two inches on its hoist (staff) by seventy-eight inches on its fly. The national color of this pair was loosely described as conforming to the design specified for the large (twenty by thirty-six foot) garrison flag. In the description of the garrison flag, the canton (the section of blue in the upper staff corner which encloses the stars) was specified to extend from the top through the seventh stripe and from the staff to a distance equal to one-third of the length of the flag. On the garrison flag, these proportions resulted in a canton that was nearly twelve feet square. However, when compressed into the nearly square proportions of the national color, the result was a canton that was decidedly rectangular—technically thirty-nine inches on the staff by only twenty-six inches on the fly.[12] The national color secured by the state for the Second Wisconsin conformed to this literal interpretation of the regulations, though shortages in the overall measurements of the flag resulted in a canton only thirty-two and a half inches on the staff by twenty-three and a half inches on the fly.

Colonel S. Park Coon, commander of the Second Wisconsin, did not trust the patriotic fervor that had furnished the First Wisconsin and so many of the volunteer companies with colors during the first few months of the war. Instead, on June 7, 1861, he assigned a nebulous "Captain Sanders" to the task of providing colors for the Second and asked the state's quartermaster general for cooperation in the venture. Three Madison business concerns furnished all that Sanders would require for the Second's national color. By June 19, he had obtained a staff for the color from Church and Hawley for $8. On the next day, an oilcloth cover to protect the flag when furled and a belt with a carrying socket for the color-bearer were purchased from Thomas Chynoweth, for $2.25 and $1.50 respectively. The more significant work, however, was delegated to Mrs. R.C. Powers, who

---

[12]U.S. War Department, *Revised United States Army Regulations of 1861. . .* (Washington, 1863), 461, paragraphs 1464 and 1466. This description was copied unchanged from the similar regulations printed in 1841, 1847, 1857, and 1861 (unrevised). Although several contractors to the New York Quartermaster's department depot consistently provided national colors with square cantons during the Civil War, the literal oversight was not corrected until 1884, when the width of the canton on the fly was officially specified as thirty-one inches on national colors.

secured the necessary materials ($5.38 for silk, $1.25 for a silk cord to secure the flag to its staff, and 25¢ for brass rings through which the cord passed), cut and sewed the material (for $12), and gilded the stars and lettering upon the flag (for $7). She was paid on June 21, and for $37.23 the Second Wisconsin had obtained a commendable color in only three weeks' time.[13]

If the flag had any short-comings, it was its size, which was approximately six inches short of regulations in both height and fly. The gilding performed by Mrs. Powers, however, not only conformed to contemporary standards, but even exceeded usual practices to permit the unit designation, "2ND REGT WISCONSIN VOL" to appear properly on both sides of the center

National color of the Second Wisconsin Infantry, 1861–1863.

stripe. (Although regulations called for embroidery, in actual practice the U.S. Quartermaster Department consistently substituted painting or gilding for embroidery in the colors it caused to be made for the Army between 1808 and 1880. Due to bleeding of the oil paints, it was usually impractical to paint lettering on both sides of the same piece of silk.) The same gilding that Mrs. Powers used for the unit designation was employed to apply the thirty-four stars to each side of the double-thick, dark blue canton. Lacking specifications, Mrs. Powers opted for a relatively simple star arrangement of seven horizontal rows of equally spaced stars. Each row had five stars, except the uppermost, which had four. Alignment with the lower stars was maintained by simply leaving a gap above the vertical row closest to the staff.

[13]Wisconsin National Guard, Quartermaster Corps, General Correspondence of the Quartermaster General (Record Group 1159), Box 2 (June 6–10, 1861), letter of Colonel S. Patrick Coon to Quartermaster General W. W. Tredway, June 7, 1861, Wisconsin State Archives. Hereinafter references to record Group 1159 are cited as Wis. QMG, Gen. Corr. The only individual of the Second with the name approximating "Captain Sanders" was Sergeant (later Lieutenant) George F. Saunders of Company D. The respective bills of Church & Hawley of June 20, 1861, Thomas Chynoweth of the same date, and Mrs. R.C. Powers of June 21, 1861 may be found in Box 2 (June 20–25, 1861).

Although the flag was provided with cord and tassels, the requirement that its edges be fringed was neglected. There is evidence that the desired fringe was not available in Madison. As it was the flag was completed only hours before the Second Wisconsin entrained for Washington, precluding even a brief presentation ceremony.[14]

The Second Wisconsin Active Militia had been called to its Madison rendezvous on April 23, 1861. On May 6, the War Department advised Governor Randall that the Second would be accepted under new quotas if it volunteered for three years rather than the initially anticipated three months. Nearly all of the assembled companies acceded to the new conditions, and on June 20 the Second Wisconsin Infantry departed Madison with its barely completed national flag in the hands of the Randall Guards (Company H). Upon reaching the "seat of the war" in northern Virginia, the Second was assigned to a polyglot brigade under the command of Brigadier General William T. Sherman. Within the month, Sherman's Brigade was marching towards a confrontation with the Confederate army near a creek called Bull Run. There, the Second would nearly lose its month-old color.

In the battle of Bull Run, Sherman's brigade was committed piecemeal. In the confusion, the Second Wisconsin (clad in gray uniforms) was fired upon from both front and rear, causing the regiment to retreat hastily. The Second was rallied near a field hospital. While attempting to reform, the color-sergeant of the Second took time to assist acting corporal George L. Hyde, who had been wounded, to the hospital. Private Robert S. Stephenson held the national color for the color-sergeant during his absence.

Before the regiment had fully reformed, an ill-advised order caused the Second to break again, this time in a panic for Washington. While retreating, Stephenson was beset by elements of Confederate cavalry. An intervening fence offered temporary haven. Rescue came, however, when two of the regimental bandsmen, Richard Carter and his brother George B. Carter, discarded their instruments for muskets and succeeded in unit-

---

[14]CWV, Vol.1, p. 82.

ing approximately fifteen Union soldiers around the threatened color.[15] Thus guarded, Stephenson and the color safely retreated.

Regimental color of the Second Wisconsin Infantry, 1861–1863 (obverse).

Regimental color of the Second Wisconsin Infantry, 1861–1863 (reverse).

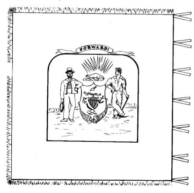

While the Second Wisconsin was recuperating from its losses at Bull Run, another flag was being prepared for it in Madison: its blue regimental color. This new flag was unique to the early Wisconsin regiments. Composed of two layers of dark blue silk, the new flag was bound on three sides with a heavy gold fringe. In full accord with regulations, the obverse (the side viewed when the staff is to the viewer's left) bore a nearly exact representation of the Great Seal of the United States, painted in gold and browns, and copied directly from the 1861 *Army Regulations.*[16] A crimson-edged gold scroll beneath the seal bore the unit designation in white letters: "2ND REGT WISCONSIN VOLUNTEERS." The two layers of silk were necessary, for the reverse side bore an entirely different design: the 1851 version of the seal of the state of Wisconsin. This seal, in full color and apparently adapted from the engraving appearing on the governor's stationery, was painted on an arced panel edged with a gold border. Surmounting the seal on a gold scroll was the state motto, "FORWARD!" in crimson letters. This use of the state seal on a field of blue as a flag preceded the official adoption of the first state flag by nearly two years.

---

[15]*Ibid.,* Vol. 1. pp. 103–104: "The Colors of the Second Regiment/The Retreat." This article was initially published in the *Milwaukee Sentinel,* August 9, 1861.

[16]*Revised United States Army Regulations of 1861...* (Washington,1863), 460. The only significant difference was the shield on the eagle's breast, which bore only stripes (nineteen), but no blue chief.

On August 2, 1861, Governor Randall visited the Second Wisconsin and presented this new regimental flag to the regiment.[17] Of the original nine-man color-party, only two had survived to receive the new flag. Joining these two individuals with the other replacements was Robert S. Stephenson.[18] For saving the national color of the regiment at Bull Run, Private Stephenson had been promoted to carry one of the two colors of the Second. He continued in this capacity through the Second Bull Run campaign of 1862. Convalescing at a field hospital at the beginning of the Maryland campaign, Stephenson roused himself from his sick bed and rejoined the Second Wisconsin on the eve of the battle of Antietam. He asked to be reassigned once more to the colors, permission was granted. On the night of September 17, his body, riddled by seven bullets, was found next to that of color-corporal George W. Holloway in the infamous Cornfield. The post of greatest honor had proved to be a post of mortal danger, as other colorbearers of the Iron Brigade would discover.

Prior to (and later as a result of) the attack upon Fort Sumter, the Wisconsin legislature had adopted several measures to enhance the preparedness of the state militia. One hundred thousand dollars was appropriated for uniforms and equipage, and a war loan of twice that amount was eventually authorized. On the basis of this legislation, Governor Randall called into state service four regiments of infantry in addition to the First and Second regiments. Randall successfully politicked to have all of these units accepted into federal service as three-year volunteers, which permitted the state to recoup the money expended in equipping and sustaining these regiments. And among the equipage of the war that the state had purchased were several colors, including those of the Sixth Wisconsin Volunteers.

The companies of the Sixth Wisconsin had been organizing since April. As the Second Wisconsin prepared to depart Camp Randall, the companies of the Fifth and Sixth regiments were called to

---

[17]CWV, Vol.1, p.118.

[18]Edwin B. Quiner, *The Military History of Wisconsin: A Record of the Civil and Military Patriotism of the State in the War for the Union* (Chicago, 1866), 453–454. Although Quiner spells the name "Stevenson," the *Roster of Wisconsin Volunteers, War of the Rebellion 1861–1865* (Madison, 1886), Vol. 1, p. 355, lists him as "Stephenson." See also CWV, Vol. 2, p. 22, wherein the death of Holloway is erroneously reported at Second Bull Run, but Stephenson's name is correctly spelled.

Presentation color of the Sauk County Riflemen, Company A, Sixth Wisconsin Infantry, 1861.

rendezvous at the Second's former barracks. The Sauk County Riflemen (soon to become Company A of the Sixth) had completed their recruiting by June 6. When the Sixth's Lieutenant Colonel Julius P. Atwood visited Baraboo to officially swear the company into state service, the ladies of the town presented the company with a small silk United States flag bearing a painted eagle in its canton.[19] It would be the only recorded flag privately presented to the Sixth. For its regimental colors, the Sixth would have to rely upon the graces of the state.

Possibly remembering the delay that had occurred between the delivery of the Second Wisconsin's national and regimental colors, Wisconsin's quartermaster general, William W. Tredway, evidently sought a source that could deliver regimental colors in a short period of time. *Army Regulations* nonchalantly described an infantry regiment's "second, or regimental color, to be blue, with the arms of the United States embroidered in silk on the centre. The name of the regiment in a scroll, underneath the eagle."[20] Given such a vague description, the only complexity lay in the rendition of the arms of the United States, either in embroidery or the traditional substitute, oil paint. Hence, on June 27, 1861, Quartermaster General Tredway addressed a letter to S.F. White & Bro. of Chicago for two such regimental flags, substituting painting for embroidery.[21] S.F. White & Bro. responded two days later, quoting a price of $45 each if fringed and $40 if not.[22] Under no great pressure to provide colors for the Fifth

---

[19]Philip Creek and Mair Pointon, *History of the Sauk County Riflemen, Known as Company "A," Sixth Wisconsin Veteran Volunteer Infantry, 1861–1865* (Baraboo, 1909), 11–12. See also CWV, Vol. 1, pp. 231–232.

[20]*Revised United States Army Regulations of 1861 ...* (Washington, 1863), 461, paragraph 1466.

[21]Wisconsin National Guard, Quartermaster Corps, Outgoing Correspondence of the Quartermaster General, 1861–1873 (Record Group 1160), Vol. 1, p. 262, Wisconsin State Archives. Hereinafter references to Record Group 1160 are cited as Wis. QMG, Letter Books. (Note: the cover titles are interchanged between volumes 1 and 2 of this record group.)

[22]Wis. QMG, Gen. Corr., Box 3 (June 26–30, 1861). Regulations called for colors to be fringed.

and Sixth regiments, Tredway apprised White on July 1 that the "colors will not be ordered at present."[23] However, in Washington the situation began to look ominous as the three-months' militia and volunteers called for in April began to muster out. Suddenly the Lincoln administration was again clamoring for troops, and Tredway was forced to hurry the outfitting of the two regiments at Camp Randall.

Anticipating national colors through a New York contract with Paton & Co., Tredway concentrated on securing regimental colors for two Madison units. On July 8, therefore, Tredway placed the following order with S.F. White & Bros.:[24]

> Please have two stand of colors made immediately for 5th and 6th Regiments Wisconsin Volunteers (one each). They must be made in accordance with the printed regulation No. 1370, page 436 (Army Regulations 1857) for infantry Regimental color, blue silk, fringe, cord & tassels & pike, all complete, and forwarded to me at this place. At one time I supposed I should not need them & so wrote you, but they are now wanted if you can furnish them as you then stated.

Three days later Tredway forwarded S.F. White an order for six and a half yards of flag fringe and badgered White to know when the colors would be completed.[25] White, however, was not a flag manufacturer, and he had let out the work to Gilbert Hubbard & Co., also of Chicago. Gilbert Hubbard & Co. acted swiftly on the order, and by July 16 had shipped the two flags via express to Madison.[26] Two days later, the Sixth Wisconsin was drawn up for review in their newly issued gray uniforms, and the blue regimental color

---

[23]Wis. QMG, Letter Books, Vol. 1, p. 328.

[24]*Ibid*, Vol. 1, p. 367. In terms of flag descriptions, the 1857 regulations were identical to those of 1861, revised.

[25]*Ibid.*, Vol. 1, p. 393.

[26]Wis. QMG, Gen. Corr., Box 4 (July 23–25, 1861), Gilbert Hubbard & Co. to Q.M. Gen. W.W. Tredway, July 25, 1861. Gilbert Hubbard & Co.'s bill of July 23, 1861, is in the same folder. This bill was returned for proper signatures and finally for correction when it was discovered that the price failed to meet the quote of S.F. White & Bro. See S.F. White & Bro. to W.W. Tredway, June 29, 1861, Box 3 (June 26–30, 1861); Gilbert Hubbard & Co. to H.K. Lawrence, July 27, 1861, Box 4 (July 26–28, 1861); and Gilbert Hubbard & Co. to H.K. Lawrence, July 31, 1861, Box 4 (July 29–31, 1861), and Wis. QMG, Letter Books, Vol. 1, pp. 464, 482, and 502.

was entrusted by Colonel Lysander Cutler to Sergeant George W. Reed of Company G.[27]

Composed of a single layer of pieced, dark blue silk, the regimental color of the Sixth Wisconsin was fringed in yellow on three sides.[28] On each side, the artist for Gilbert Hubbard & Co. had executed in oils a full-color rendition of the seal of the United States—the eagle predominately in brown tones and grays, the shield in red and white stripes under the blue chief and bordered in gold, the arrows in gold and the laurel in green in opposing talons, the sky behind the eagle's head a sunburst fading to a gray-blue sky studded with white stars and surmounted by a purple and gray cloud. From the eagle's beak flowed a red scroll bearing the motto "E PLURIBUS UNUM" in black letters. A simple light-red scroll, edged with gold, bore the gilded lettering "6ᵀᴴ WISCONSIN REGIMENT" in an arc below the seal and completed the painted designs. What model may have served as the artistic basis for this rendition of the U.S. seal is enigmatic, as a multitude of variations had found their way into print by the middle of the nineteenth century. Clearly the artist was not influenced by the stiff, unnatural eagle depicted in *Army Regulations*. His interpretation of the bird on the regimental color of the Sixth Wisconsin, and on other early colors purchased from Gilbert Hubbard & Co. in 1861 and early 1862, was far more relaxed and lifelike.[29]

Regimental color of the Sixth Wisconsin Infantry, 1861–1863.

[27]Diary of Sergeant Levi B. Raymond, Company G, Sixth Wisconsin, for 1861, entry of July 18 (manuscript in private collection, Des Moines, Iowa). George W. Reed was furloughed in February of 1862 to attend his dying child. When he failed to return he was declared a deserter, effective April 14, 1862; see Raymond diary for 1862, entries of February 18, 19, 22, and 23. In addition to Sergeant Reed, five others were assigned to the colors at Camp Randall: Corporal Mamory V. Smith (Company B), Corporal Mathew Keogh (Company D), Corporal Andrew G. Deacon (Company E), Corporal Hirman B. Merchant (Company H), and Corporal William A. Remington (Company K). See CWV, Vol.1, p. 235; General Orders No. 5, Sixth Regiment Wisconsin Active Militia, July 12, 1861. See also p. 236 of the same volume.

On July 28, 1861, just four days after the Fifth Wisconsin had departed for Washington, the Sixth Wisconsin followed her sister regiment. The Sixth left with but a single flag, the blue regimental color presented by the state ten days earlier. The national color had failed to materialize. However, with the organization and equipage of the Seventh and Eighth regiments, the state would rectify its failure to furnish that national color.

On July 23, 1861, the U.S. War Department authorized Wisconsin to complete the organization of the two additional active militia regiments that the Wisconsin legislature had established at Governor Randall's urging. Although the governor had not planned to call the Seventh and Eighth regiments into camp until after the fall harvest, the Union defeat at the battle of Wilson's Creek in Missouri prompted the War Department to press Governor Randall for an earlier rendezvous. Wisconsin's quartermaster general therefore began to arrange for the equipping of these two new units. On August 20, 1861, an order was confirmed with Gilbert Hubbard & Co. that provided flags not only for the two new regiments, but also for the Sixth regiment's lack of a national standard as well. Deputy Quartermaster General Means' order was succinct, stating in part:[30]

> Please send us at as early a day as possible one Regimental color (blue Silk) for 8th Regm't Wis. Vol., army regulation in all respects,
>
> And three national Colors, Silk, regulation size, 6ft. 6in. by 6ft., marked on the middle stripe as following:
> One of them— 6th Regt. W.V.
> 7th Regt. W.V.
> 8th Regt. W.V.
>
> The last two with staff, spearhead, cords & tassels; 6th Regm't col. all compl. except staff. . . .

---

[28]The flag measures sixty-eight inches on its staff by seventy-five inches on its fly, exclusive of the three-inch-deep silk fringe bordering three of its sides.

[29]Wis. QMG, Letter Books, Vol. 2, pp. 232, 266, and 650, and Vol. 4, p. 14. Between September 26, 1861, and April 4, 1862, Wisconsin's Quartermaster General ordered sets of colors from Gilbert Hubbard & Co. for the reorganized First and the Ninth, Tenth, Eleventh, Twelfth, Thirteenth, Fourteenth, Fifteenth, Sixteenth, Seventeenth, Eighteenth, and Nineteenth regiments. All were basically of the same pattern, although the artist who executed the eagle on the colors of the Fifteenth executed it in a more heraldic form. All these regimental colors bore the motto "FORWARD" upon them.

Apparently these flags were delivered by the sixth of September.[31] Rather than ship the national color of the Sixth via express, Quartermaster General Tredway devised a less expensive shipping procedure. On September 16, he informed Colonel Cutler of the Sixth Wisconsin: "I send per hands of Qr. Master H.P. Clinton of 7th Wis. Regt. your National color. You can have them mounted in Washington & this department will pay the bill upon presentation." A closing note informed Colonel Cutler that the Seventh would depart in two days.[32]

The national colors provided by Gilbert Hubbard & Co. under Means' order conformed to the regulations with but a single deviation: the use of gold paint where silver embroidery was officially specified. This gilding was used in both the application of the unit name, "6TH REG T WISCONSIN VOLUNTEERS.", to the center stripe and the thirty-four stars in the canton. These gold stars were arranged into six horizontal rows, the topmost and the bottom rows containing five stars each, the four center rows six stars each. Like the regimental colors provided by Gilbert Hubbard & Co. up to this time, the flag was secured to its staff by means of silk ties that passed through four small brass grommets equally spaced in the hemmed leading edge of the flag.[33]

National color of the Sixth Wisconsin Infantry, 1861–1863.

---

[30]*Ibid.*, Vol. 1, pp. 540 and 602. The national colors of the Seventh and Eighth regiments had previously been ordered on August 8 by Assistant Quartermaster General H.K. Lawrence. The bill for these flags amounted to $198 ($50 for the complete regimental flag of the Eighth, $45 each for the national colors of the Seventh and Eighth regiments, and $40 for the national flag of the Sixth without pole or tassels). An additional $18 was charged for lettering the three national colors; see Wis. QMG, Gen. Corr., Box 5 (August 1–5, 1861), bill of Gilbert Hubbard & Co.

[31]Wis. QMG, Letter Books, Vol. 2, p. 23. On that day the national flag of the Eighth Wisconsin was examined and returned for corrections and the bill of September 5, misdated August, was acknowledged.

[32]*Ibid.*, Vol. 2, p. 105.

[33]From the surviving fragments, the flag appears to have measured seventy-one inches on its staff by at least seventy-two inches on the fly, exclusive of the four-inch-deep buff silk fringe. The canton measured thirty-eight inches on the staff by twenty-four inches on the fly. Only "VO" of VOLUNTEERS remains on the center stripe.

So, like the Second Wisconsin, the Sixth was a belated recipient of its full complement of colors.

In placing the order with Gilbert Hubbard & Co. on August 20, 1861, for the colors required for the Sixth, Seventh, and Eighth regiments, no mention was made for a regimental color for the Seventh Wisconsin. For reasons not clear, the state had decided to have that flag made in Madison. On August 1, 1861, a voucher was issued to Mrs. R.C. Powers of Madison for one "Regimental Color" and the "Silk & Trimmings for Regimental color for 7th Reg't."[34] Audited twenty days later, Mrs. Powers' payment included $15.00 for actual sewing of the flag, $20.00 for painting on the color, and $19.61 for "Silk & trimmings for same."[35] The last amount did not include the six and a half yards of fringe or the cords and tassels. These had been ordered from S.F. White & Bro. of Chicago on July 11, but they had not been received by August 1. As with earlier flag orders, S.F. White & Bro. had subcontracted the order to Gilbert Hubbard & Co., who finally delivered the yellow silk fringe and the blue and white cords and tassels on August 6.[36] The completed flag was issued to Quartermaster Henry P. Clinton of the Seventh during the last week of September.[37]

Although conforming to the vague specifications of *Army Regulations*, the painted U.S. seal and the scroll beneath it on the regimental color of the Seventh were unlike any design heretofore provided by either Gilbert Hubbard & Co. or any of the other suppliers of flags to Wisconsin during the Civil War. In lieu of the traditional frontal view of a shielded eagle with upright, extended wings, the regimental color of the Seventh depicted a side view of a crouched eagle with partly folded wings. Moreover, rather than supporting the shield on its breast, the gold and brown eagle was perched upon the shield (which had the additional irregularity of having white stars upon the blue

[34]Wisconsin National Guard, Quartermaster Corps, Return of Property Purchased and Issued by the Quartermaster General for the Year Ending August 1, 1862 (Record Group 1163), Abstract A, Wisconsin State Archives.
[35]Wis.,QMG, Gen. Corr., Box 5 (August 1–5, 1861), voucher 629, and Box 5 (August 21–26, 1861), amended voucher 629.
[36]Wis. QMG, Letter Books, Vol. 1, pp. 393, 501, and 540. See also Wis. QMG, Gen. Corr., Box 6 (August 6-10, 1861), bill of Gilbert Hubbard & Co.
[37]The Return of Property Purchased and Issued by the Quartermaster General for the Year Ending August 1, 1862, cited above (Record Group 1163), Abstract A, indicates a receipt date of September 28, but Abstract E lists an issue date of September 21. The latter date is undoubtedly correct, since the Seventh departed Madison on that date.

Regimental color of the Seventh Wisconsin Infantry, 1861–1863.

chief.) A gold scroll, edged red along its upper border but blue on the lower portion, emanated from the eagle's beak, bearing the national motto in black lettering. A panoply of flags (including the U.S. flag) protruded from behind the eagle's lowered, golden head, all surmounted by nineteen scattered, silver stars. Although distinctive, the design was not unique. Rather it was copied (with the minor modification of the scroll) from a popular motif that had been utilized on several contemporary printed objects, including at least one widely distributed guide to commercial signal flags.[38] Beneath these devices the artist had painted a curling white and red rococco scroll bearing the unit's name abbreviated in gilt figures and letters, shadowed red, low and to the viewer's right.[39] Although much of the paint has flaked off, it is not so nearly damaged as its matching national color.

Originally believed to be of regulation size, no more than two-thirds of the national color of the Seventh Wisconsin survives. Any fringe it may have had has been torn away. The canton, which originally bore thirty-four gold stars (thirty set in double ellipse—probably ten in an inner ring surrounded by twenty in a concentric outer ring—with one other star set in each corner of the canton) is badly damaged.[40] Surprisingly, no evidence of a unit abbreviation appears on the center stripe or any of the other surviving fragments.[41] The star pattern (so different from

---

[38]Henry J. Rogers, *Rogers American Code of Marine Signals. . .* (Baltimore, 1855), title page.

[39]The color, exclusive of the two-and-a-half-inch-deep yellow silk fringe, measures sixty-nine and three-quarters on its staff by seventy-one and a half inches on its fly. The painting, applied identically to each side of the single layer of dark blue silk, has mostly flaked away.

[40]As an alternative star pattern, the inner ring may have had only nine stars, with a corresponding gap at the top or bottom of the ring; in that case the thirty-fourth star graced the center of the canton.

[41]The surviving fragments measure approximately seventy-one and a half inches on the staff by fifty-five (of the presumed seventy-eight) inches on the fly, inclusive of the two-inch-diameter sleeve that held the flag to its original staff. The canton measures thirty-six inches on the staff by twenty-four inches on the fly, and the stars that remain each are two and a half inches across their points.

***National color of the Seventh
Wisconsin Infantry, 1862–1863.***

those upon the national flags of the Sixth and Eighth regiments ordered August 20, 1861) as well as the absence of any painted unit abbreviation indicates that the national flag of the Seventh carried from at least mid-1862 until November of 1863 was not the color ordered from Gilbert Hubbard & Co. and delivered on September 5, 1861, with the regimental color of the latter regiment.[42] Instead, the flag exhibits the characteristics of several eastern flag manufacturers who served the Philadelphia U.S. Quartermaster's Depot and several eastern states.

Since it is convincingly established that the pair of colors secured for the Third Wisconsin was purchased by Colonel Charles S. Hamilton in Philadelphia,[43] a strong possibility exists that the Seventh may have turned to the Philadelphia market for a new color in early 1862. Did Colonel Joseph Van Dor of the Seventh take the original national color home with him as a souvenir when he resigned on January 30, 1862? Documentary evidence strongly indicates that the Seventh had two colors when it left Madison in 1861.

On September 17, 1861, the state's Military Store Keeper recorded the receipt of *two* "Belts for Color Bearers" for the Seventh regiment.[44] These belts had been ordered on the sixteenth from Thomas Chynoweth of Madison at the cost of $4 by Assis-

---

[42]Wis QMG, Gen Corr., Box 5 (August 1–5, 1861), bill of Gilbert Hubbard & Co. See also Wis. QMG, Letter Books, Vol. 2, p. 32, Quartermaster General Tredway to Gilbert Hubbard & Co., September 6, 1861.

[43]The colors of the Third Wisconsin exhibit the same artistic characteristics as those furnished the Regular Army prior to the Civil War. The painting of the colors for the Regular Army had regularly been subcontracted to Samuel Brewer of Philadelphia prior to hostilities.

[44]Wisconsin National Guard, Quartermaster Corps, Military Store Inventory, 1861 (Record Group 1173), p.234, Wisconsin State Archives. The date of receipt is erroneously listed as September 7, instead of September 17; however, the date of issuance is correctly given as September 19, 1861.

tant Quartermaster N.B. Van Slyke.[45] These two belts were issued to the Seventh upon a requisition, dated September 19, that also included "1 sett Regimental Colors" and "1 staff & Trimmings for U.S. colors."[46] The set of regimental colors referred to was that furnished by Mrs. Powers of Madison. This staff for "U.S. colors" is enigmatic. Although firm documentation is lacking, it was probably procured from Church & Hawley of Madison, who consistently supplied the state with marker poles and who had furnished the Fifth regiment with a "large Flag Staff" for $6 in July for its national color.[47] Additional expenses relating to the staff for "U.S. colors" included $1 for plating the mountings[48] and $2.50 for cords and tassels.[49] Since Gilbert Hubbard & Co. had already provided a set of the latter on August 6 for the regimental color made by Mrs. Powers for the Seventh Wisconsin, and since the national color sent to the state on September 16 by the same firm for the Seventh was billed as "all complete with fringe, Pole &c.," the flag staff requisitioned on September 19 was apparently for some other flag. And, though a faint possibility exists that the staff and its trimmings may have been for the national color that the Seventh carried to Washington for the Sixth regiment, the dating of the bills and their continued association to the Seventh regiment strongly suggest that it was for some other U.S. flag of the Seventh, possibly a presentation color.

After the Seventh Wisconsin entrained for the East on September 21, a brief stop was made at Stoughton, home of the Stoughton Light Guard, the Seventh's Company D. The state papers reported that the ladies of that town "had made a fine banner to present to the Stoughton company, but finding that under the regulations it would be only an encumbrance if carried, did not present it."[50] On the other hand, this had not de-

---

[45]Wis. QMG, Gen. Corr., Box 6 (September 16–18, 1861), N.B. Van Slyke to Thomas Chynoweth, September 16, 1861, and voucher for total payment of $5.88, dated September 18, 1861.

[46]*Ibid.*, Box 6 (September 19–21, 1861), voucher 4, Abstract K, receipted to Quartermaster Clinton of the Seventh Wisconsin.

[47]*Ibid.*, Box 4 (July 29–31, 1861), account with Church & Hawley, audited July 30, 1861—entry of July 6.

[48]*Ibid.*, Box 6 (September 19–21, 1861), bill of E. Detwiler of Milwaukee, and Box 6 (September 1–5, 1861), "Abstract of supplies shipped to Gen. W.W. Tredway, Q.M. Gen. for 7th Regt. W.V. by Col. James Holton, Asst. Q.M.G.," encompassing "1 spear or color Head for 7th Regt. &c. for plating sent Express Sept. 9, 1861."

[49]*Ibid.*, Box 5 (August 21–26, 1861), bill of S.F. White & Bro.

[50]CWV, Vol.1, p. 266: "Progress of the 7th Regiment to Chicago—Its Reception There."

terred the Grand Rapids Union Guards (Company G) from bringing along the national flag that had been presented to them.[51] By inference, there clearly was no need for another national flag in the Seventh Wisconsin when it departed Madison. Nevertheless, when the Seventh joined Brigadier General Rufus King's Brigade

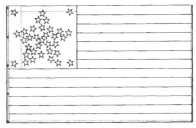

Presentation color of the Grand Rapids Union Guards, Company G, Seventh Wisconsin Infantry, 1861.

near Washington on October 1, 1861, a soldier of the Sixth Wisconsin would record: "The 7th Wisconsin arrived here last Tuesday. Our boys and thos of the 2d made extravagant demonstrations of delight when they saw the grey uniforms and *blue flag* coming up the road from towards Washington. . . ."[52]

What had become of the Seventh's national color? In view of the real danger of being fired upon by Union forces because of their gray uniforms, it seems incredible that the Seventh would have gone to war without it. But the reason for its absence, like the flag itself, is lost to history.

Under these six colors, the Wisconsin contingents of the Iron Brigade would fight their first major engagement together at Gainesville (more recently called the battle of Brawner Farm), cover the retreating Army of Virginia at Second Bull Run, storm Turner's Gap at South Mountain, and capture and lose the Cornfield at Antietam on the bloodiest single day of the war. With the addition of the Twenty-fourth Michigan, they would protect the Army of the Potomac's flank at Fredericksburg, brave the Confederate sharpshooters at Fitz Hugh's Crossing, and skirmish at Chancellorsville. The flags would be torn by musketry and shell fragments, the staffs scarred by well-aimed bullets. By 1863, battle and the elements had reduced the flags of the Iron Brigade to tatters. Of course, the problem was not restricted to

---

[51]The presentation flag of the Grand Rapids Union Guards is part of the collections of the State Historical Society of Wisconsin, accession no. 51.214 (H2038).

[52]The emphasis on *blue flag* is the author's. CWV, Vol. 1, p. 259, "from the Sixth Regiment," letter of "L.B.R." [Levi B. Raymond, Company G], October 4, 1861.

the flags of the Iron Brigade. By the middle of the war, the flags that the state had purchased in 1861 for other Wisconsin volunteers were also in need of replacing.

For example, at the battle of Perryville, Kentucky (also called the battle of Chaplin Hills by the Union participants), on October 8, 1862, the First Wisconsin Infantry suffered staggering casualties protecting the left flank of the Union Army of the Ohio from wave upon wave of Confederate assaults. The colors of the First were riddled, and its staff was struck twice. Of the color-party, only three were unscathed when night ended the battle. When the color-sergeant fell, grievously wounded, a private, James S. Durham of Company F, grasped the flag and kept it aloft. Despite it losses, at one point the First Wisconsin counterattacked, capturing the battleflag of the First Tennessee Volunteers and dragging the abandoned guns of the Fourth Indiana Battery to safety. In appreciation of these actions, the Indiana artillerymen presented the First Wisconsin with a set of colors that included a new national and regimental color as well as a small marker.[53] The receipt of these new colors permitted the First Wisconsin to retire the battle-worn national color it had received from the state in October of 1861. On January 19, 1863, Colonel John C. Starkweather returned the First's national color to Governor Edward Salomon with an eloquent letter of transmittal that was later published in the Madison *Journal*.[54]

Starkweather's account struck a chord in the patriotic spirit of State Senator Benjamin F. Hopkins, a Republican representing Wisconsin's Twenty-sixth Senatorial District. On February 16, 1863, Hopkins begged the indulgence of the senate to suspend the rules in order to introduce a resolution establishing a joint committee commissioned with the responsibility of establishing a state flag and preparing legislation that would permit Wisconsin regiments to substitute this new flag for their worn-out colors.[55] Hopkins' resolution carried both houses, and a five-man committee headed by Hopkins was created to translate his recommendations into appropriate legislative form.

---

[53] Quiner, *Military History of Wisconsin*, 429.

[54] CWV, Vol. 8, p.84: "Flag of the First Wisconsin—A Glorious Souvenir."

[55] State of Wisconsin, *Journal of the Senate, Annual Session A.D. 1863* (Madison, 1863), 299–300; *Journal of the Assembly of the State of Wisconsin, Annual Session, A.D. 1863* (Madison, 1863), 276–277. See also the *Milwaukee Sentinel*, February 17, 1863.

The five-man joint committee deliberated less than a month on the design for the state flag. On March 13, the committee reported the following proposal for the design of Wisconsin's state flag:[56]

> To be of dark blue silk, with the arms of the State of Wisconsin painted or embroidered in silk on the obverse side, and the arms of the United States, as described in paragraph 1435, of 'New Army Regulations,' painted or embroidered in silk, on the reverse side. The name of the regiment, when used as a regimental flag, to be in a scroll, beneath the State arms.
>
> The size of the regimental colors to be six feet six inches fly, and six feet deep on the pike. The length of the pike for said colors, including spear and ferrule, to be 9 feet and 10 inches. The fringe yellow; cords and tassels blue and white, silk intermixed.

This proposal was adopted by the senate on the sixteenth and by the assembly the next day. On March 25, 1863, it officially became Joint Resolution No. 4 of that year.[57]

Although parroting much of the descriptive language for the blue regimental color prescribed by then current *Army Regulations*, the design of the flag was attributed by the *Milwaukee Sentinel* "to the good taste of Secretary Watson."[58] (The *Sentinel* may have been basking in it's own glory, since William H. Watson had been both an editor and co-owner of the paper before joining Governor Randall's staff, first as his personal secretary in 1858 and then in 1861 as his military secretary.) Although documentary evidence fails to support or deny the *Sentinel's* contention, Secretary Watson would be instrumental in securing the new flags for the state in 1863. Documentary evidence does indicate that he envisioned a double-layered flag like that which

---

[56] *Journal of the Senate...1863*, p. 502.

[57] *Ibid.*, p. 570, and *Journal of the Assembly...1863*, p. 587; *Journal of the Senate...1863*, pp. 548, 617,and 645, and *Journal of the Assembly...1863*, p.688. See also *Acts of a General Nature, Passed by the Legislature of Wisconsin at the Extra Session in the Year 1862 and at the Annual Session in the Year 1863, Together with Joint Resolutions and Memorials Passed at Said Annual Session* (Madison, 1863), 483.

[58] *Milwaukee Sentinel*, March 17, 1863.

the state presented to the Second Wisconsin in August, 1861.

In addition to the resolution establishing the state flag, Hopkins' joint committee submitted a bill that authorized the governor to purchase flags in accordance with the state flag resolution. Submitted to the legislature on March 20, the bill quickly passed the procedural hurdles. Signed by the governor on April 2, 1863, the bill became Chapter 215 of the Laws of 1863.[59]

This new "act to authorize the governor to purchase flags" essentially encompassed three provisions, one of which prescribed the procedure for paying for the flags. In substance, regiments having worn-out flags that had been provided by the state were to requisition a new set through the governor. The new set would include a state flag conforming to the provisions of the newly adopted joint resolution of the legislature together with a national color bearing the names of the engagements in which the unit had served "honorably." The new set of colors could only be purchased with the proviso that the unit's old colors be returned to Wisconsin for safekeeping.[60]

The progress of the bills on the new state flag and the procedures for acquiring them evidently were common knowledge to the officers commanding the Wisconsin contingents of the Iron Brigade. Only two days after the act permitting the governor to provide flags was officially in effect, Colonel Bragg, commanding the Sixth Wisconsin, determined to take advantage of the law's provisions and wrote the governor:[61]

> On behalf of the regiment I have the honor to command, I return to the state of Wisconsin the regimental color presented this regiment in the summer of 1861.
>
> We part with it reluctantly, but its condition renders it unserviceable for field service. When we received it, its folds, like our ranks, were ample and full; still emblematical of our condition, we return it, tattered and torn in the shock of battle. Many who have defended it, 'sleep the sleep that knows no waking';

[59]*Journal of the Senate..1863,* pp. 582, 648, 711, 715, 762, 766, 808, 834, 837, and 840; *Journal of the Assembly...1863,* pp.862, 882, and 964.
[60]*Acts of a General Nature...1863,* pp. 347–348.
[61]Dawes, *Service with the Sixth Wisconsin,* 130, 131. The national color was retained by the regiment.

they have met a soldier's death; may they live in their country's memory.

The regiment, boasting not of deeds done, or to be done, sends this voiceless witness to be deposited in the archives of our State.

History will tell how Wisconsin honor has been vindicated by her soldiers, and what lessons in Northern courage they have given Southern chivalry. If the past gives any earnest of the future, the "Iron Brigade" will not be forgotten when Wisconsin makes up her jewels.

The flag itself accompanied newly appointed Major John F. Hauser on his brief leave to Wisconsin. The Madison *Journal* reported Hauser's arrival at Madison on April 17:[62]

Major Hauser, of the 6th Regiment delivered today at The Executive Office, the old regimental flag of the gallant Sixth regiment, worn and torn, and tattered in the fierce conflicts of Gainesville, Bull Run, 2nd, South Mountain, Antietam, and Fredericksburg. It will be replaced by the Governor with a new flag under the law passed by the late session.

Although the Second Wisconsin would retain its colors until actually replaced by a new set, Colonel Lucius Fairchild must have made application for a replacement stand of colors at about the same time as the Sixth. The first sets of colors ordered under the 1863 legislation included sets of flags for the First Wisconsin, the Sixth Wisconsin (both of which regiments had returned one of their 1861 colors), and the Second Wisconsin.

The governor was directly responsible for securing new colors for the Wisconsin regiments under the 1863 law, but the details of procurement befell to his military secretary, William H. Watson. Watson sought bids for the new flag only four days after the enabling act was formally published. On April 14, 1863, Military Secretary Watson addressed identical

<hr>

[62]*Milwaukee Sentinel*, April 17, 1863.

letters to G.D. Norris & Co. of Milwaukee and Gilbert Hubbard & Co. of Chicago, stating:[63]

> I am directed by the governor to enquire your prices for National and Regimental Flags. Under a recent act of the Legislature, he is authorized to furnish new flags to such of our regiments as shall require them, having used up their first flags in service. The National Colors are to be the U.S. Regulation style, and to be inscribed with the names of the battles in which they have been borne. The Regimental flags to be also as described in paragraph 1438 of Army Regulations, except that it must, I suppose, be of double silk, so as to have the State Arms painted on their obverse side. We shall need several at once, and probably ten or more of each. Your early reply, with prices &c. will oblige.

Gilbert Hubbard & Co. responded by suggesting that a single layer of silk could be employed if the painting of the arms of Wisconsin and the United States could be executed upon opposite sides of a single panel centered on the blue field of the state flag. Anxious that the work be executed in Wisconsin, Watson suppressed any scruples he may have had about the ethics of his action and communicated the essence of Gilbert Hubbard & Co.'s bids to Norris on April 21, noting:[64]

> Your letters of 17th and 21st are received. We have an offer to make the flags needed, in good style 'complete with pole, spear head, fringe, tassels, cover, and boot' for $85 and $60. This presumes the regimental flags to be of single silk, having a panel painted, so as to put a coat of arms on [sic] each side. This is more desirable than to have it of double silk. The parties propose to commence delivery in two weeks from the order. Time is an important element, as two of our regiments are without any flags whatever, and must be supplied at once. The Governor will await a letter from you tomorrow before deciding upon this order.

---

[63]Department of the Executive, Administrative, Letter Books-General (Record Group 33), Vol. 9, pp. 39 and 40; Wisconsin State Archives. Hereinafter cited as Wis. Gov., Letter Books.
[64]*Ibid.*, Vol. 9, p. 76.

In fact, Secretary Watson waited a full week in hope of channeling the state's orders to the Milwaukee firm, but the delay was to no avail. Finally, on April 28, Watson placed the following order with Gilbert Hubbard & Co. of Chicago:[65]

> I am directed by the Governor to order from you at present, six each of the Regimental and National flags, as per your proposition—complete at $85 and $60. The National Flag to be the U.S. regulation, and a portion of them to be lettered on the stripes. The Regimental Flags to be as per enclosed extract from the recent act of the Legislature. The words to be inscribed on the National Flags and the designations of regiment for the scroll in the others will be sent in a few days. You will oblige by proceeding with the work as rapidly as possible.

Watson complied with his promise to forward the designations and battle honors on May 2, but only for four of the sets under preparation—those of the First, the Second, the Sixth, and the Twenty-third regiments. (The last regiment had never received colors from the U.S. Quartermaster Department, so the governor had decided to furnish one of the newly ordered sets to it and bill the federal government for the expenditure.) The other two sets of colors ordered on April 28 were to be held in abeyance until the commanding officers of the units for which they were destined provided a proper listing of the battle honors which the units had earned.[66]

Gilbert Hubbard & Co.'s proposal had optimistically indicated a delivery schedule of two weeks. However, by May 26, a month had passed since the order for the six sets of colors had been placed, and no flags had yet been received. Accordingly, Watson asked when the colors might be forthcoming. His inquiry produced results, for by June 4, four flags—two full sets—had been received at Madison, though without the required slings and sockets.[67] These were the sets for the First Wisconsin and the

---

[65] *Ibid.*, Vol. 9, p. 109.
[66] *Ibid.*, Vol. 9, p. 127, and Vol. 10, p. 185. The two remaining sets were respectively designated and lettered for the Eighteenth Wisconsin and Twenty-ninth Wisconsin on instructions forwarded respectively August 1, and August 10, 1863; see Vol. 10, pp. 81, 148, and 185. See also Wis. QMG, Letter Books, Vol. 4, pp. 462 and 464, relative to the billings for the colors of the Twenty-Third and Twenty-ninth regiments.
[67] Wis.Gov., Letter Books, Vol.9, pp. 284 and 337.

Second Wisconsin. Two days later Watson forwarded both sets to their respective regiments. Colonel Fairchild was notified of the shipment in a separate letter:[68]

> Under the provision of a law of the last session of the Legislature [wrote Watson], a new stand of colors for your regiment has been prepared and forwarded by Express to Washington, to take the place of those which have been worn out in the service. Your regiment will doubtless part with regret with the glorious old flags beneath which it has won so high a reputation, and around which its brave officers and men have so often rallied, and poured out their blood like water in the contest with the enemies of the Union and Constitution; but those flags, returned to this state, will be guarded with care, and serve as mementoes of your valor. The new stand of colors is entrusted to you, in full confidence that the men of the gallant old 'Second' will never suffer them to be disgraced, but will return under them to receive the grateful thanks of their fellow citizens.

The colors of the Sixth Wisconsin were ready a few weeks later, and on June 25, a similar letter notified Colonel Bragg of the shipment of his new set of colors:[69]

> Colonel:
> In compliance with your request a new set of colors for your regiment has this day been sent by Express to Washington in place of those whose torn & bloodstained folds attest the heroism and bravery of your noble regiment. Upon the new regimental [sic—actually the national] flag you will find inscribed the names of the battles in which the regiment won its proud name fighting under the colors that will now be preserved in the archives of our State as a perpetual monument of the patriotism, bravery & heroism of the 6th Reg. Wis. Vols.

---

[68] *Ibid.*, Vol. 9, p.347. See also p. 348 for Acting Governor James T. Lewis' similar letter of June 6, 1863, to the commander of the First Wisconsin regiment.
[69] *Ibid.*, Vol. 9, pp. 450–451.

With full confidence that the honor of our country &
state will be as nobly protected by you & your regiment
under the new colors as it has been under the old, I
remain.

very respectfully yours,

EDWARD SALOMON
Governor of Wisconsin

In spite of these June mailings, the new sets of flags would not
participate in the Iron Brigade's next encounter with the Confederate Army of Northern Virginia—the sanguinary struggle on
the ridges west and north of Gettysburg, Pennsylvania.

On June 12, 1863, the Iron Brigade and the rest of the reorganized First Army Corps left their camps along the Rappahannock
River in Virginia in pursuit of their old adversary. General Robert E. Lee had slipped his Army of Northern Virginia around the
flank of the Army of the Potomac and had launched an invasion
of Pennsylvania. For the rest of the month, still under their old
colors, the Iron Brigade marched northward in search of the
elusive foe. The morning of July 1 found the brigade nearing
the crossroads hamlet of Gettysburg. To the northwest, Union
cavalry was attempting to delay Confederate General Henry
Heth's Division, which was advancing from the Northwest on
the Chambersburg Pike. Brigadier General Lysander Cutler's
Brigade, in the Union vanguard, quickly relieved the cavalry-
men north of the Pike. The Iron Brigade followed close behind
to forestall the enemy advance southward towards Gettysburg.
The old colors of the Iron Brigade were due one last bathing in
shot and shell, smoke and blood.

The veterans of the Iron Brigade advanced into the fray. They
struck Brigadier General James J. Archer's Brigade of Ala-
bama and Tennessee troops just as they were regrouping from
their crossing of a little creek called Willoughby Run. In the
onslaught, Archer's Brigade was shattered, and Archer himself
was captured by the Second Wisconsin, which led the charge.
The Second had entered the battle with a reduced color-party.
Philander B. Wright, a sergeant detached from Company C,

carried the national color. An unidentified corporal carried the blue regimental state color. Only two corporals had been detailed as their color-guard. In the initial assault against Archer's Brigade, this entire color-party fell dead or wounded. When the colors fell, Corporal Rasselas Davison of Company H sprang forward and raised the regimental color, and Corporal Paul V. Brisbois of Company G seized the national color from the wounded Wright. (Miraculously, both men survived the three-day battle unscathed.) By the end of the day, when the Second Wisconsin made its final stand on Seminary Ridge against the onslaught of Major General William D. Pender's Confederate Division, the color-company, Company H, had been so reduced by casualties that Major John Mansfield assigned its survivors to act as a color-guard for Davison and Brisbois.[70]

The Seventh Wisconsin joined the initial assault on Archer's Brigade in echelon to the left of the Second Wisconsin. Less exposed than the rest of the brigade, the colors of the Seventh suffered less severely until the retreat through Gettysburg late in the afternoon. Sergeant Daniel McDermott of Company K carried the Seventh's national color on July 1. With the collapse of the Union forces north of the town, the Iron Brigade was forced to retreat hastily through Gettysburg to the formidable hills to the south. Colonel William W. Robinson of the Seventh, commanding the brigade after the wounding of his superiors, reported that McDermott "was wounded just as we were entering the town, retiring, by a charge of grape and cannister, the same charge shivering the flag-staff into a number of pieces. McDermott was placed upon a caisson that was moving ahead of us, still hanging to the tattered banner, which he waved in defiance at the foe as he rode off. He has carried this color through every battle in which the regiment has been engaged."[71] That night, bivouacked on Culp's Hill, the color-party of the Seventh substituted a sapling for the shattered staff of its national color.

In the disjointed assault across Willoughby Run, the Nineteenth Indiana had adjoined the left of the Seventh Wisconsin. It carried two colors. The blue regimental color was carried by Cor-

---

[70]Mary A. Livermore, *My Story of the War: A Woman's Narrative of Four Years Personal Experience as Nurse in the Union Army, and in Relief Work at Home, in Hospitals, Camps, and at the Front, During the War of the Rebellion*...(Hartford, Connecticut, 1889), 61–62; *OR*, Series I, Vol. 27, Pt.1, p. 275; and Captain R.K. Beecham, *Gettysburg: The Pivotal Battle of the Civil War* (Chicago, 1911), 88.
[71]*OR*, Series I, Vol. 27, Pt. 1, p. 281.

poral David Phillips and dated to 1861, when it had been presented to the regiment by ladies of Indianapolis.[72] The complementary national color presented to the Nineteenth in 1861 had been retired during the winter of 1862–1863 at the instigation of Indiana Governor Oliver P. Morton, who replaced it with a national color requisitioned from the U.S. Quartermaster Department but decorated with the unit name

Presentation regimental color of the Nineteenth Indiana Infantry, 1861–1864.

by the state.[73] Sergeant Burlington Cunnigham, of the Nineteenth's Company K, carried this flag into the assault upon Archer's Brigade.

Sergeant Cunnigham, who had saved the old national color of the regiment at Antietam, unfurled the national color as the Nineteenth Indiana charged across Willoughby Run, only to receive a bullet through his left side from the first Confederate volley. The same volley wounded P.J. McKinney of Company B, serving as one of the color-guard. When Cunnigham fell, Abram J. Buckles picked up the national color and pressed forward. Afterward, Buckles was surprised to discover that Cunningham had not only survived his wound but felt sufficiently recovered to renew his claim to carry the national colors!

[72]David I. McCormick, comp., and Mindwell Crampton Wilson, ed., *Indiana Battle Flags*...(Indianapolis, 1929), 78–81, 105–107, and 378. The characteristics of this flag suggest that it was manufactured for the presentation by Baldwin's Fancy Bazaar of Indianapolis.

[73]Judging from other colors issued at the same time, the Nineteenth's second national color was a standard U.S. Quartermaster's contract flag of the type purchased through its New York Depot from Paton & Co. and William and Alexander Brandon. These colors were distinguished from the colors purchased through the Philadelphia Depot by having square cantons, decorated with gold stars in five horizontal rows—7,7,6,7,7. On November 25, 1862, the *Indianapolis Daily Journal* published the text of a circular headed "Executive Department/ Indianapolis, Nov. 22, 1862" in which Governor Morton informed unit commanders that replacement colors could be procured through him. Telegrams dated December 3 and 4, 1862, concern the shipment of the Nineteenth's new national color on the "24th," presumably of November, 1862; see [Governor Oliver P. Morton], "General Telegrams and Dispatches," No. 9 (September 30–December 31, 1862), Indiana State Archives. Presumably this color was decorated by the state with the inscription "19TH REG T INDIANA VOLS." in gold Roman figures and letters on the red stripe below the canton. However, when later viewed by its bearer, he stated that "there is no letters on it except a few that is in paint, the gilt letters are all gone; there was very little by which I could identify it to a certainty." See Burr M. Clifford to H.C. Marsh, December 3, 1915, in the Marsh Papers, Indiana State Library.

The two remaining brigades of Heth's Confederate Division soon renewed their attack, bringing the color party of the Nineteenth Indiana under a withering fire. Sergeant Cunningham was wounded again, this time in the leg. Buckles was wounded in the shoulder. Color Corporal Phillips, carrying the regimental color, was surprised to suddenly find himself alone and unhurt next to his stricken fellow flag-bearer, Blair. Unhesitatingly he took up both flags. He raised the national color and waved it briefly; then Phillips too was wounded, falling upon both flags.

As the Nineteenth Indiana fell back to a new position, someone called to Captain W.W. Macy that the colors had fallen. Captain Macy, Lieutenant Crockett East, and Burr M. Clifford (who had been detailed to the color-guard shortly before the battle) rushed back to the place where Corporal Phillips had fallen and rolled him off the flags. As Lieutenant East attempted to encase one of the flags, he was killed, but Captain Macy and Private Clifford succeeded in furling the colors and were bringing them to the rear when they encountered Sergeant Major Asa Blanchard. Blanchard accosted the two and demanded possession of the flags. Macy at first balked, but Colonel Samuel J. Williams interceded on Blanchard's behalf, and Blanchard uncased the national color and began to rally the regiment with it. Then he too was struck, the bullet severing an artery in his thigh. Dodging spurts of Blanchard's life-blood, Private Clifford took up the national color and safely retreated with it to Cemetery Hill, where the Union forces rallied.[74]

Initially posted on the Iron Brigade's left flank, the Twenty-fourth Michigan carried but a single color into battle at Gettysburg.[75] The flag, a beautifully embroidered national color, had been made by Tiffany & Co. of New York City and presented to the regiment on behalf of F. Buhl & Co. of Detroit on August 26, 1862. Upon receiving the color, Colonel Henry A. Morrow noted that Color Sergeant Abel G. Peck would shortly receive a check from a Detroit citizen and, to ensure the flag's safety, an additional $100 was guaranteed Peck if the flag was

---

[74] *The Press* of Muncie, Indiana, October 8, 1908; Burr M. Clifford to H.C. Marsh, February 20, 1911, in the Marsh Papers.

[75] O.B. Curtis, *History of the Twenty-fourth Michigan of the Iron Brigade, Known as the Detroit and Wayne County Regiment* (Detroit, 1891), 225–227, describes the ceremonies of April 27, 1864, when this old color was replaced by two new flags: a national color under the charge of Sergeant George R. Welch and a regimental color carried by Thomas Saunders, protected by eight other corporals.

returned unsullied by Rebel hands.[76] Sergeant Peck never had the opportunity to claim that reward. In the attack across Willoughby Run, a Confederate bullet made him the first of at least nine color-bearers to fall beneath the banner of the Twenty-fourth Michigan on July 1, 1863.

Presentation national color of the Twenty-fourth Michigan Infantry, 1862–1864.

With Peck's death, Corporal Charles Bellore, detailed to the color-guard from Company E, sprang forward and took up the colors. In the blazing fight between J. J. Pettigrew's Brigade of North Carolinians and the Iron Brigade for McPherson's Ridge, Corporal Bellore was killed and Private August Ernest of Company A assumed Bellore's charge. Ernest held fast to the colors until he too was killed. Sergeant E.B. Welton of Company H picked up the flag from the fallen Ernest and gave it to Colonel Morrow, who searched in the confusion for survivors from the color-guard. But Corporal William Ziegler of Company A was already dead and Corporal Thomas Suggett of Company G and Private Thomas B. Ballou of Company C lay mortally wounded. Finally he found Corporal Andrew Wagner of Company F, the last man of the color-guard, and to him he entrusted the flag. Wagner waved the flag for several minutes and then was shot through both lungs. Colonel Morrow again took the colors, but Private William Kelly of Company E intervened, saying, "The Colonel of the Twenty-fourth Michigan shall not carry the colors while I am alive." He had just grasped the staff when a bullet killed him instantly. Colonel Morrow then turned the flag over to Private Lilburn A. Spaulding of Company K., but he soon retrieved it to help rally the retreating regiment as it fell back towards Gettysburg. While endeavoring to reform the Twenty-fourth Michigan, Morrow was wounded in the head and forced to leave the field. Temporarily blinded by his own blood, he turned the colors to an unidentified enlisted man, who safely brought the color to Seminary Ridge, though himself mortally wounded. From the hands of this prostrate, unknown soldier,

---

[76]*Ibid.*, 40–41.

Captain Albert M. Edwards, the only senior officer of the Twenty-fourth to survive the day's carnage, took the color and brought the remnants of the regiment to the safety of Cemetery Hill.[77] There rallied the remnants of the Iron Brigade, including the Sixth Wisconsin.

The Sixth had been detached from the rest of the brigade early on the morning of July 1. The color-bearers of the single national color remaining with the Sixth Wisconsin were to share the fate of the flag bearers who strove to keep the colors flying through the storm of musketry that swept McPherson's and Seminary ridges west of Gettysburg. Like the final color-bearer of the Twenty-fourth Michigan, however, their names would not be recorded for posterity. All of them fell, their faces to the enemy, during the headlong counterattack of the Sixth Wisconsin at a railroad cut just north of the Chambersburg Pike.

When the rest of the Iron Brigade attacked and crushed Archer's Brigade, the Sixth Wisconsin and approximately 100 detached men from all of the regiments comprising the brigade provost guard were withheld as a reserve on Seminary Ridge. While the Iron Brigade successfully counterattacked the brigade of Heth's Division south of the Chambersburg Pike, General Cutler's Second Brigade of the First Division, north of and astride the pike, was driven back by the attacks of Confederate General Joseph R. Davis' Brigade. Soon this Confederate brigade outflanked the position held by the Iron Brigade and the left units of Cutler's Brigade. The Sixth Wisconsin, in reserve, was called upon to fill the gap. Supported by New York troops, the men of the Sixth Wisconsin plunged into the maelstrom.

In the moments it took to traverse the 150 yards from the Chambersburg Pike to the railroad cut, no one recorded the names of the color-bearers who bore the flag of the Sixth. Writing after the war, Lieutenant Colonel Rufus R. Dawes, who commanded the Sixth, remembered:[78]

---

[77] *Ibid.*, 164–166; see also Morrow's report of February 22, 1864, in *OR*, Series I, Vol. 27, Pt. 1, pp. 268–269.
[78] Dawes, *Service with the Sixth Wisconsin*, 168.

...The only commands I gave as we advanced, were, 'Align on the colors. Close up on the colors. Close up on the colors!' The regiment was being so broken up that this order alone could hold the body together. Meanwhile the colors fell upon the ground several times, but were raised again by the heroes of the colorguard. Four hundred and twenty men started in the regiment from the turnpike fence, of whom about two hundred and forty reached the railroad cut.

First Lieutenant Earl M. Rogers, of Company I of the Sixth, recalled after the war:[79]

. . .The distance to the cut was but a few hundred yards and the Mississippians were firing as rapidly as they could load. The colors of the Sixth fell, Dawes seized them and carried them forward. Soldiers eager to be in the vortex of battle rushed to carry the flag when it went down a second time. Dawes again lifted the colors and gave the command to close on the colors. Again men rushed to seize the flag in that great conflict to carry it to the railroad cut.

Although Lieutenant Rogers remembered the names of eleven of his compatriots of Company I that fell in the charge, regrettably he could name none of those who carried the colors except Colonel Dawes.

For the balance of July 1, the Sixth Wisconsin fought to the right of the positions occupied by the rest of the Iron Brigade. Though it had suffered less severely than the rest of the brigade, when its withdrawal ended at Cemetery Hill that night only five men huddled around the national color. Sixty others straggled in over the next twenty-four hours, so that the unit was considered sufficiently strong to serve as the brigade's floating reserve at Culp's Hill during the next two days of the battle. On the night of July 2, an enterprising Confederate endeavored to capture the flag of the Sixth shortly after an assault against the Union lines on Cemetery Hill had been repulsed. He was seen by the Wisconsin men, and Sergeant George Fairfield of Company C later remem-

[79]Earl M. Rogers to J. A. Watrous, undated typewritten manuscript, in "Civil War Materials," Box 2, in the J.A. Watrous Papers, State Historical Society of Wisconsin.

bered the rebel's fate: "He fell back, pierced with six balls and a bayonet."[80] This brave, futile gesture would prove to be the last threat to any of the old colors of the Iron Brigade during 1863. Battered as the units they represented, the colors were ready for retirement. New faces and new flags would start the 1864 campaigns of the Iron Brigade.

The new sets of colors that had been ordered by the state in April and sent in June to the Second and the Sixth regiments finally caught up with the regiments in early August of 1863. The flags had been sent to Washington, D.C., for delivery by the state's military agent there, W.Y. Selleck. By mid-July he had succeeded in locating the brigade in Maryland and informed the unit commanders of the arrival of the flags. Lieutenant Colonel Rufus Dawes of the Sixth noted in a letter on July 16:[81]

National color of the Second Wisconsin Infantry, 1863–1864.

> . . .The State of Wisconsin has at last furnished us a beautiful stand of colors upon which our battles are inscribed: 'Rappahannock, Gainesville, Bull Run, South Mountain, Antietam, Fredericksburg, Fitz Hugh's Crossing, Chancellorsville, Gettysburg,' and who can tell what more is in store for this shattered fragment of veteran heroes before next July when our term of service will expire.

The battles that Dawes related were indeed the engagements in which the Sixth had participated, but they did not actually reflect what he had seen upon the flags, which had not yet arrived. The flags finally caught up to the two Wisconsin regiments on August 2. Writing from Beverly Ford on the Rappahannock

---

[80]George Fairchild to J.A. Watrous, undated manuscript, in "Civil War Materials," Box 2, in the Watrous Papers.

[81]Dawes, *Service with the Sixth Wisconsin*, 187–188.

River in Virginia on the day before the flags' anticipated arrival, Dawes commented:[82]

> The State of Wisconsin has sent us a fine stand of colors which will, I understand, be here to-morrow. I wish I could keep our old color lance, which has three bullet holes through it, and two other marks. Think of that slender stick struck five times. . . .

Five days later, on August 5, Dawes provided a better insight as to the actual engagements appearing on the flag when he wrote that he had "sent away our old flag yesterday, and were sorry to see it go. The new one is a very handsome silk color (national color) and it has all of our engagements inscribed upon it, except Fitz Hugh's Crossing."[83]

The national flag to which Dawes referred survived only as fragments. The ravages of the elements and of the 1864 campaigns (and possibly souvenir hunters) reduced this flag to a small section of the stripes of the upper, fly corner. Given the similarity between the state colors received by the Second and Sixth at the same time, it is highly probable that the national colors were likewise nearly identical except for the unit number and addition of the battle honor "BULL RUN, JULY 1861" to the listing of the Second's engagements.

Basically conforming to the measurements specified by *Army Regulations* for national colors,[84] the new U.S. color of the Second Wisconsin bore thirty-four gold stars painted on its rectangular canton, set in six horizontal rows—6,5,6,6,5,6. The unit name, "2ᵈ Wisconsin Infantry Volunteers.," was painted in gold block letters on the center stripe, the upper-case letters three and a quarter inches high and the lower-case two inches high. The first red stripe beneath the canton bore the battle honors that had been painted in gold by the artist working for Gilbert Hubbard & Co. Since the order for these flags had been placed

---

[82] *Ibid.*, 193–194.

[83] *Ibid.*, 195.

[84] Exclusive of the two-and-a-half-inch-deep yellow silk fringe that borders all but the staff edge, the 1863–1864 national color of the Second Wisconsin measures seventy-one inches on its staff by seventy-three inches on its fly. Its rectangular canton measures thirty-seven inches on the staff by twenty-six inches on the fly, and the thirty-four gold stars thereupon each measure two and five-eighths across their points. The flag was attached to its staff by means of a sleeve, two and a quarter inches in diameter, formed by doubling over the leading edge, lining it with linen, and sewing it to form a tube.

in April, they reflected the 1861 and 1862 battles of the Second. To fit the stripe, the honors were compressed into two horizontal rows. The upper row bore the names "BULL RUN, JULY, 1861. GAINESVILLE, BULL RUN, AUG, 1862." and the lower "SOUTH MOUNTAIN, ANTIETAM, FREDERICKSBURG.," all in one-and-a-half-inch-high lettering. On the red stripe beneath the stripe bearing these honors, two additional honors were added: "CHANCELLORSVILLE." over "GETTYSBURG." Although painted in the same height and face of lettering as the earlier honors, the coloration and widths of individual letters suggest that these last two honors were affixed to the flag after it left Gilbert Hubbard & Co. Most likely these two honors were added in Washington through the efforts of agent Selleck, possibly accounting for the August delivery of the two sets of colors.

The complementary state flags accompanying the national colors received by the Second and Sixth regiments in August were

State regimental color of the Second Wisconsin Infantry, 1863–1864 (obverse).

nearly identical. Essentially they agreed with the provisions of the 1863 joint resolution of the legislature as modified in the Hubbard company's proposal of April. Each blue silk color bore a disc in its center, approximately thirty to thirty-two inches in diameter, inclusive of the three-eighths-inch-wide edge. Against a sky blue background circumscribed by gray clouds, the obverse side of each bore a painted rendition of the 1851 Wisconsin coat of arms. The buff shield with Wisconsin's symbols dominated the center, surmounted by a badger crest in natural colors and a red scroll with the state motto "FORWARD" in the same yellow paint that edged the scroll. To the right of the shield stood a sailor holding a coiled rope and attired in dark blue except for his white shirt with light-blue falling collar and plastron. Leaning against the shield's left side was a bareheaded yeoman with a pick, wearing a loose red shirt and black trousers. Natural-colored cornucopiae emptied at the foot of the shield. On the reverse, the background coloration remained the same. However, in lieu of Wisconsin's coat of arms, the national coat of arms

State regimental color of the Second Wisconsin Infantry, 1863–1864 (reverse).

was displayed. Like some of Gilbert Hubbard & Co.'s earlier work, the source for the representation remains enigmatic. The eagle was displayed with wings upstretched and with a flowing red scroll bearing the motto "E PLURIBUS UNUM" curling in front of the eagle's right wing and neck but behind its left wing. The clipped corners on the U.S. shield on the eagle's breast were atypical of the era when the flag was painted. Three gold arrows in the eagle's left talons and a natural-colored olive branch in its right talons completed the design of the panel on the reverse side.

On each side beneath the painted panels bearing the coats of arms, the regimental designation was painted on a single-piece, six-inch-wide red scroll edged in gold. For the Second, this unit name read "2D WISCONSIN INFANTRY VOLS.," and for the Sixth the number was changed so that it read "6TH WISCONSIN INFANTRY VOLS." in gold letters and figures.[85] Unlike the lettering on the national colors (which read correctly only on the obverse of the flag), these abbreviations were readable from both sides of the flag.

The receipt of these two sets of colors prompted the commanding officers of the Second and the Sixth regiments to return their war-torn colors to the state in accordance with the provisions of the 1863 state legislation. Colonel Rufus Dawes of the Sixth Wisconsin addressed state agent W.Y. Selleck at Washington August 4, sending back the U.S. color:[86]

---

[85]Less the two-and-a-half-inch-deep yellow silk fringe, the blue silk state flags of the Second Wisconsin and the Sixth Wisconsin respectively measure seventy and three-quarters inches on the staff by seventy-six inches on the fly and seventy-one inches on the staff by seventy-three inches on the fly. Both flags were attached to their staffs by means of sleeves, formed as described above.

[86]Dawes, *Service with the Sixth Wisconsin*, 195.

> I have the honor to acknowledge at the hands of Mr. Taylor, the receipt of the National color, with the names of our battles inscribed upon it, provided by the State of Wisconsin for this regiment. I send to you herewith for transmission to the Governor our old color. It can no longer be unfurled and five bullets have pierced the staff. Its tattered folds and splintered staff bear witness more eloquently than words to the conduct of the men who have rallied around it from Gainesville to Gettysburg. We send it to the people of Wisconsin, knowing what they expect of us, and we promise that the past shall be an earnest of the future, under the beautiful standard they have sent us.

While the Sixth sent their colors through Washington, the Second sent their colors directly to Wisconsin, where they arrived on August 13. When the latter's colors passed through Milwaukee en route to Madison, the *Milwaukee Sentinel* commented that the "battle flags of the Second Wisconsin arrived here yesterday of the United States Express, and were sent directly on to Madison. They are completely riddled with bullets, and one of the staffs showed marks of having been hit some four or five times, and splintered by balls."[87]

In spite of the condition of these flags, the state was loath to retire them. Accordingly, the national colors of the Second Wis-

National color of the Sixth Wisconsin Infantry, 1863–1864 (reconstruction).

State regimental color of the Sixth Wisconsin Infantry, 1863–1864 (obverse).

---

[87] *Milwaukee Sentinel*, August 14, 1863.

State regimental color of the Sixth Wisconsin Infantry, 1863–1865 (reverse).

National color of the Seventh Wisconsin Infantry, 1863–1865.

consin and the Sixth Wisconsin were loaned in October of 1863 to the Great Northwestern Soldiers Fair in Chicago, to be displayed in the "relic" section of this huge fund-raising event. There both were photographed in their tattered condition.[88] "Sanitary fairs" in 1864 and 1865 would call the old flags to further service. Meanwhile, Wisconsin's Iron Brigade contingents still possessed one dilapidated set of colors. The Seventh Wisconsin would shortly rectify that problem.

Although documentation is lacking, the receipt of the new colors of the Second and Sixth regiments must have elicited both admiration and envy within the Seventh Wisconsin, for shortly after their receipt, the Seventh requisitioned a new set of state colors. On September 9, 1863, Military Secretary W.H. Watson placed the following order with Gilbert Hubbard & Co. of Chicago:[89]

> I am directed by the Governor to order of you a suite of flags for our 7th Reg't Infantry Volunteers; the National Flag to be inscribed as follows:
>
> | | |
> |---|---|
> | Gainesville | Fredericksburg |
> | Bull Run, 1862 | Fitzhugh Crossing |
> | South Mountain | Chancellorsville |
> | Antietam | Gettysburg. |

For some reason, this set of colors took nearly two months to prepare. Finally, on November 7, 1863, Secretary Watson wrote to Wisconsin's Washington agent, W.Y. Selleck: "I am directed

---

[88]*Ibid.*, October 30 and November 14, 1863.
[89]Wis. Gov., Letter Books, Vol. 10, p. 361.

by the Governor to say that he sends by Express today the new flags for the 7th Wis. Inf'y, to your address. You will oblige the Governor by seeing that they are delivered to the regiment, and that the old flags are sent to the Governor immediately."[90] It is not known if these new colors reached the Seventh before the commencement of the Mine Run Campaign three weeks later.

State regimental color of the Seventh Wisconsin Infantry, 1863–1865 (obverse).

State regimental color of the Seventh Wisconsin Infantry, 1863–1865 (reverse).

The blue state flag that accompanied the Seventh's new set of colors differed little from those issued in June to the Second and Sixth Wisconsin regiments. However, certain details were altered by the artist who executed the state coat of arms. The shape of the scroll bearing the state motto, "FORWARD," was modified from a single section to a double-section ribbon. The entire coat of arms was also made somewhat smaller, and the gray clouds that adjoined the gold edge of the panel were made more pronounced. The single-piece red scroll below the coat of arms bore the regimental designation "7TH REGT. WIS. INFANTRY VOL'S." in gold lettering.[91] The shape of the scroll was identical to that used earlier on the flags of the Second and the Sixth.

While this state color differed little from the six predecessors that had been ordered in April,

---

[90] *Ibid.*, Vol. 10, p. 675

[91] The blue state color of the Seventh Wisconsin received in 1863 measures seventy-one inches on its staff by seventy-two inches on its fly, not including the two-inch-deep yellow silk fringe on three sides. The central disc is about twenty-eight inches in diameter, inclusive of its one-half-inch gold edge. The scroll is four and three-quarter inches wide, also inclusive of its one-half-inch gold edge. The sleeve is two inches in diameter when flattened.

the Seventh's new national color was different in two important respects. West Virginia's admission to the Union had become official July 4, 1863, and from that day hence until 1865 the national flag bore thirty-five stars. The new national color of the Seventh reflected that addition. The thirty-five gold stars in the rectangular dark-blue canton were arranged in six horizontal rows—6,6,5,6,6,6. The unit abbreviation on the center stripe also had been modified in style of lettering and method of ordering the wording. The latter apparently followed the form used on the state color. And, while much of the lettering has been lost to age and battle damage, the new style apparently eliminated the use of lower-case lettering in favor of all upper-case letters.[92] (This was also done on the new national flags ordered for the Tenth Wisconsin on August 14 and for the Eleventh Wisconsin on October 9, 1863.)[93] The eight battle honors specified in the original order to Gilbert Hubbard & Co. of September 7 were painted on the red stripe below the canton in two horizontal rows in one-and-three-quarter-inch gold letters, shadowed black low and left. The Wisconsin contingents of the Iron Brigade at last all had new colors.

While the Wisconsin units of the brigade were the only regiments to receive new colors until 1864,[94] another elabo-

---

[92]The 1863–1865 national color of the Seventh Wisconsin measures seventy-one inches on its staff; however, only fifty-seven inches remain of what is presumed to have been a seventy-six-inch-long fly, all exclusive of the two-and-a-half-inch-deep yellow fringe on three sides. The flag is heavily damaged, so that only the "7th R" remains of the unit designation, and several of the battle honors are partly or completely missing as well. The canton, measuring thirty-eight inches on the staff by twenty-six inches on the fly, is also damaged, but the star pattern is discernible. Regrettably, the restorer of this flag incorrectly reapplied the unit abbreviation and one of the battle honors during conservation of the flag.

[93]For the orders to Gilbert Hubbard & Co. for the colors of the Tenth Wisconsin (as well as one for the Seventeenth) and the Eleventh Wisconsin, see Wis. Gov., Letter Books, Vol. 10, p. 185 and 516.

[94]The Twenty-fourth Michigan received a new set of colors on April 27, 1864; see Curtis, *History of the Twenty-fourth Michigan*, 225–227. Unfortunately, these flags were not restored during Michigan's Civil War Centennial Restoration Program, so their design and measurements remain enigmatic. Major William Orr of the Nineteenth Indiana applied to the state adjutant general for a new national color on September 8, 1864, stating that "the staff is shattered by balls and the flag itself torn to shreds by balls and the elements." See telegram, Indiana State Archives. Six weeks later the Nineteenth Indiana was consolidated with the Twentieth Indiana, so the newly requisitioned color never saw combat with the Iron Brigade. By the time the Twenty-fourth Michigan received a new state flag on February 22, 1865, it too was no longer part of the Iron Brigade. See Curtis, *History of the Twenty-fourth Michigan*, 296.

rate flag was presented to the Iron Brigade as a whole in 1863. Shortly after the battle of Gettysburg, and partly in recognition of the gallant conduct of the brigade in that battle, a group of citizens of Wisconsin, Indiana, and Michigan residing in Washington determined to honor the brigade through the gift of a special presentation flag.[95] The group raised a thousand dollars and commissioned the New York City Firm of Tiffany & Co. to prepare the flag of the richest practical construction, which was to be presented with great pomp at a special ceremony.[96] The first anniversary of the battle of Antietam (September 17, 1863) was selected

Mathew Brady's photograph, taken prior to the September, 1863, presentation of the Tiffany embroidered Iron Brigade color, depicts the flag in its full glory.

as the appropriate presentation date, and dignitaries were invited to make preparations for that date. Unfortunately for these dignitaries, Major General George Meade, commander of the Army of Potomac, had other plans, and the Iron Brigade moved to Culpepper, Virginia. Wisconsin's military agent, W.Y. Selleck, caught up with the brigade at Culpepper, and in the absence of the scheduled dignitaries, gave a speech on behalf of former Governor Randall and then presented the flag to the brigade. Colonel William W. Robinson, still commanding the brigade in the absence of wounded senior officers, accepted the gift, and then all attending officers opened the champagne that had been bought for the occasion.[97] With few exceptions, the officers of the brigade and their guests (and any enlisted men who chanced to scavenge a bottle) were happily tight that night.

The Iron Brigade flag itself was made of the finest blue silk, bordered with a deep gold fringe. In brocade embroidery in its

---

[95]Cullen B. "Doc" Aubery, *Recollections of a Newsboy in the Army of the Potomac, 1861–1865* (n.p., n.d.), 45, 164.

[96]Dawes, *Service with the Sixth Wisconsin*, 205–206; Cheek and Pointon, *Sauk County Riflemen*, 80. The latter work erroneously dates the occasion as September 19, 1863.

[97]CWV, Vol. 8, pp. 154–157. See also Curtis, *History of the Twenty-fourth Michigan*, 201–204.

WHi (x3) 17094

The field and staff officers of the Second Wisconsin Infantry, photo-
graphed at Fredericksburg, Virginia, in July of 1862. To the right is
the blue regimental color presented to the Second Wisconsin Infan-
try by Governor Alexander Randall on August 2, 1861. The tricolored
flag (white-red-blue) with the numeral "2" on the left is the regimen-
tal designating flag adopted in June of 1862.

center, the artisans at Tiffany had worked a representation of an
eagle with upstreched wings perched upon a U.S. shield floating in a bank of clouds. A shaded yellow scroll bearing the U.S.
motto, "E PLURIBUS" and "UNUM" in brown block letters flowed
from the eagle's talons and below the clouds. The entire central
device was based on the engraving appearing on the obverse
side of the $10 demand note issued by the Treasury Department
in 1861.[98] Above this central motif, similarly embroidered in yel-
lows and browns, was another scroll bearing the name "IRON
BRIGADE." Six smaller yellow scrolls decorated the edges of
the field; the three along the staff edge were respectively inscribed (top to bottom) "GAINESVILLE.," "BULL RUN.," and
"SOUTH MOUNTAIN." The three along the fly edge were similarly inscribed "ANTIETAM.," "FREDERICKSBURG.," and
"GETTYSBURG." The names of the five western regiments of
the brigade were also embroidered on the blue field, but in
yellow script figures and letters directly upon it. The upper edge
bore the designations "2nd Wisconsin." and "6th Wisconsin." The
lower edge was similarly inscribed "19th Indiana." and "7th Wisconsin." The final name, "24th Regt Michigan Vols.," was worked
into the field beneath the scroll bearing the U.S. motto. In typi-

---

[98]Robert Friedberg and Jack Friedberg, *Paper Money of the United States: A*
Complete Illustrated Guide with Valuations, Seventh Edition (New York, 1972), 29.

cal Tiffany style, a narrow sleeve along the leading edge of the flag held an iron rod that screwed into the finely finished, silver-mounted staff. In workmanship and elegance, the flag was unsurpassed.

The question arose, however, as to the role of this presentation flag. Technically the only flags permitted at brigade headquarters in the field were the designating flags ordered by the headquarters of the Army of the Potomac. Like company flags, the brigade presentation flag was therefore superfluous. The officers of the Iron Brigade resolved to send the flag to one of the Northern states for safekeeping. Since Wisconsinites outnumbered the others, the flag was sent to Madison.[99] The only flags carried at brigade headquarters into combat would be the white-red-blue horizontal tricolor that designated the 3rd Brigade of King's Division in 1862 and the white triangular pennant bearing the red disc of the First Division, First Army Corps, adopted in 1863 and associated with all the Iron Brigade's battles, even those from the 1864 campaigns.[100]

Many historians consider the Iron Brigade's gallant stand on the first day at Gettysburg as signaling the brigade's unofficial demise. Casualties incurred that day did unalterably change the "all-western" composition of the brigade. But the addition of the small First Battalion New York Sharpshooters (as well as

---

[99]Some time prior to 1919, the brigade flag was vandalized by a souvenir hunter who slashed an approximately eighteen-inch square from the lower section, including not only the "n. Vol:" of the Twenty-fourth Michigan's inscription but also the "7th Wiscon" of the Seventh Wisconsin's inscription. Prior to its presentation, the flag had been photographed by Brady's Washington studio, so a record of its original appearance survives. See Hosea W. Rood, *A Little Flag Book* (Madison, 1919), 13, for a view of the vandalized flag.

[100]The earlier brigade flag, a five-foot hoist by six-foot fly rectangular flag composed of three horizontal bars (from the top, white-red-blue) was adopted under a circular issued June 19,1862, from the headquarters of the Department of the Rappahannock; see *OR*, Series I, Vol. 51, Pt. 1, p. 683. Each regiment of the brigade had a similar flag with the numeral "1", "2", "3", or "4" laying on its side sewn to the upper white bar; however, there is no evidence to indicate that these flags were carried into combat. In a photograph taken near Fredericksburg, Virginia, in July of 1862, the flag of the Second Wisconsin of this type (bearing the numeral "2") flies near Colonel O'Connor's tent and the Second's regimental flag. For a detailed discussion of these regimental flags, see Howard Michael Madaus, "McClellan's System of Designating Flags, Spring–Fall, 1862," in *Military Collector and Historian*, 17: 1–14 (Spring, 1965). In May of 1863, a new system of distinguishing the subordinate levels of the Army of the Potomac was devised. Under this system the brigade received a white triangular flag bearing a red disc, which it continued to carry to the end of the war. See *OR*, Series I, Vol. 25, Pt. 2, pp. 152 and 469–471, and Frederick P. Todd, *American Military Equipage, 1851–1872*, (Providence, 1977), Vol. 2, pp. 318–331.

temporary assignments of other "eastern" units) was more than offset on April 28, 1864, when the Seventh Indiana was transferred to the Iron Brigade. Moreover, even though the First Army Corps was consolidated into the Fifth Army Corps in March of 1864, through August the old divisional integrity was maintained. Even after consolidation with the "Junior Bucktail" brigade in September, 1864, attrition and terminations of service affected the brigade more dramatically than the attachment of any "eastern" units.

The partially revitalized Iron Brigade entered the spring campaign of 1864 in good spirits and with new colors flying over four of its old regiments. But the first two days of combat in the Wilderness campaign (May 5 and 6, 1864) leached the strength of the brigade once more. Those two days cost the Iron Brigade more than five hundred casualties.

One of these casualties was Abram J. Buckles, who was subsequently awarded the Congressional Medal of Honor. After recovering from the wound he suffered at Gettysburg, Buckles had been appointed color sergeant of the Nineteenth Indiana. He later recalled that after the Iron Brigade had driven the enemy through a clearing in the heavily forested Wilderness, it stopped to reform.[101]

> . . .Meanwhile the Johnnies crossed the clearing and posted themselves in a dense thicket. Up to this time I had been unable, because of the bushes and trees, to unfurl my colors, but on coming into the clearing I loosened its folds and shook the regiment's flag free to the breeze. From their covered position the enemy had begun to pour a withering fire into us; comrades were dropping at every hand and delay was fatal, while retreat was never dreamed of. The only possible safety lay in a charge, and believing that a short, quick rush with such a line as we had, a heavy one, would force the Confederates to fly, I ran to the front. Waving the flag above my head, I called upon the boys to follow. To a man they responded, and together we

---

[101]"He Kept His Colors Flying," in W.F. Beyer and O.F. Keydel, eds., *Deeds of Valor: How America's Heros Won the Medal of Honor* (Detroit, 1903), Vol.1, pp. 316–317.

dashed toward the troublesome thicket. We were going in fine style when I was struck, shot through the body. I fell, but managed to keep the flag up until little John Divelbus, one of the color-guard and as brave a man as ever lived, took it out of my hands, to be killed a few minutes later.

The Wilderness would also cost the Nineteenth Indiana its commanding officer, Colonel Samuel J. Williams, who had earlier played a part in the struggle for the Nineteenth's colors at Gettysburg.

The Second Wisconsin would also lose field officers in the Wilderness: Colonel John Mansfield, who was wounded and captured, and Lieutenant Colonel William L. Parsons, who was twice wounded and missing in action. The forty casualties suffered by the Second Wisconsin caused the unit to be assigned to divisional provost guard duty for the balance of its term. Then, because it failed to secure enough re-enlistments to become a "veteran" regiment, the Second was mustered out of service at Madison on June 18, 1864. Captain George H. Otis, the unit's last commander, turned over the regimental colors to the state of Wisconsin on July 1, 1864, with these words:[102]

> The 2nd Regiment Wisconsin Volunteers having been mustered out of service upon expiration of term of service, it becomes my duty to return to the State the colors borne in the engagements on the Rappahannock and Mine Run, 1863, the first and second days battles of the Wilderness, at Laurel Hill and Spotsylvania, and to the 11th of June in the present Virginia campaign.
>
> . . . The records [of the regiment] are our story and the colors the mementoes of our firm resolve of the right and a will to do and dare when facing a common foe. I only regret that I cannot give the names of the color bearers who have fallen in our three years' service. Yet I may assure you they were always in good hands, and defiantly waved in the face of the enemy.

---

[102]George H. Otis (and Alan D. Gaff, ed.), *The Second Wisconsin Infantry* (Dayton, 1984), 11.

Throughout 1864 the other color-bearers in the Iron Brigade seldom received official recognition.

On the second day of the battle of the Wilderness (May 6, 1864), Colonel Rufus Dawes of the Sixth found it necessary to again take up the unit's colors to rally the regiment.[103] The name of the color-bearer who carried it up to that point was not recorded. Similarly, the color sergeant who was wounded carrying the colors of the Sixth in the disastrous assault at Petersburg on June 18, 1864, remains anonymous. The next casualty, however, was Sergeant C.A. Winsor of Company A, who was slightly wounded on August 19, 1864, at the Weldon Railroad battle.[104]

These sergeants had been carrying the national color of the Sixth Wisconsin. The state color drew its share of enemy fire as well, as evidenced by the bullet hole that passed directly through its staff. While no losses are recorded among the color-bearers of the state color of the Sixth, on June 12, 1864, Mair Pointon was detached from Company A to the color-guard and assigned the responsibility of carrying the state color.[105]

Compared to its mate, the state color issued to the Sixth Wisconsin in 1863 is in good condition. Aside from the hole in the staff and the corresponding damage inflicted upon the flag from the splinters, there is little to indicate that the state color saw extensive combat. The relatively good condition of the state flags of both the Sixth and the Seventh Wisconsin suggests that both may have been retired from active combat at the beginning of the siege of Petersburg. Indeed, in the autumn of 1864 the state color of the Sixth was formally retired, and by October 26 it was in the hands of the state's quartermaster general.[106] The state flag of the Seventh Wisconsin was similarly returned before the beginning of the spring campaign of 1865, the quartermaster general noting its return on March 16, 1865.[107] In the last engagements of the Seventh, only a national color was car-

---

[103]Dawes, *Service with the Sixth Wisconsin*, 251.
[104]Cheek and Pointon, *Sauk County Riflemen*, 116 and 132.
[105]*Ibid.*, 112.
[106]Wis. QMG, Letter Books, Vol. 4, pp. 691–697. The Quartermaster General evidently assumed responsibility for the returned colors of Wisconsin regiments on May 18, 1864, as those exchanged in 1863 are receipted under that date in his compiled listing of flags sent to the 1865 Chicago Sanitary Fair.
[107]*Ibid.*, Vol. 4, pp. 691–697.

ried, under the care of Sergeant George W. Davis of Company C.[108] Even the Twenty-fourth Michigan had reverted to carrying a single color. When Colonel Morrow reorganized his color-guard on December 16, 1864, he appointed only a single color-bearer, Sergeant Charles D. Durfee of Company C, protected by a truncated guard of only five corporals.[109] By the last year of the war, the surviving veterans traveled more lightly than they had in 1861, and no doubt had fewer illusions about the importance of flags, martial music, and ceremony.

Until January of 1864, when the responsibility for procuring colors was turned over to the state quartermaster general, the governor of Wisconsin had purchased for the state regiments ten full sets of national and state colors, two national colors unaccompanied by state flags, and a single state flag conversely unaccompanied by a national flag. Most of these were purchased under the authority of the act of the legislature passed on April 10, 1863. (These included the three sets received by the Wisconsin regiments of the Iron Brigade in 1863.) However, one of the sets purchased in 1863 had been paid for out of the governor's contingency fund, and three other sets were billed to the federal government.[110]

To rectify the deficiencies of the 1863 legislation, a bill had been introduced into the state senate in February, 1864.[111] However, before this proposal would pass the legislative hurdles, Governor James T. Lewis had endeavored to secure new state colors for the Wisconsin regiments returning to the state on veteran furlough. He attempted to secure these flags from the U.S. Quartermaster Department. When the latter declined to furnish anything other than colors that agreed with U.S. regulations, the governor unsuccessfully appealed to the Secretary of War.[112] Undaunted by this rebuff, Lewis appealed to ex-Gover-

---

[108]Quiner, *Military History of Wisconsin*, 480. The report cited by Quiner is not published in the *Official Records*.

[109]Curtis, *History of the Twenty-fourth Michigan*, 284.

[110]Wis. Gov., Letter Books, Vol. 10, pp. 81, 148, 185, 339, 361, 421, 516, and Vol. 11, p. 126, 241–242; Wis. QMG, Letter Books, Vol.4, pp. 462, 464, 469, and 484. See also *Annual Report of the Quartermaster General of the State of Wisconsin for the Fiscal Year Ending September 30, 1863* (Madison, 1864), 847–848, and *Annual Report of the Quartermaster General of the State of Wisconsin for the Fiscal Year Ending September 30, 1864* (Madison, 1865), 421.

[111]*Journal of the Proceedings of the Senate of Wisconsin during the Session for the Year 1864* (Madison, 1864), 100.

[112]Wis. Gov., Letter Books, Vol. 12, p. 270, and Department of the Executive, Administrative, Letter Book—Special (Record Group 34), Vol. 1, p. 217, Wisconsin State Archives.

nor Alexander Randall, who was then serving as Lincoln's Assistant Postmaster General. Randall interceded on Lewis' behalf on October 3. Though Quartermaster General Montgomery C. Meigs thought the changes could be effected with little additional expense, Lincoln's Chief-of-Staff, General Henry W. Halleck, objected. Accordingly, on October 27, Randall was informed that the U.S. would only furnish colors in accordance with current *Army Regulations* and only inscribed with honors that had been approved by the commanding officers of field armies.[113]

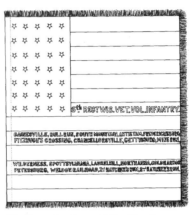

National color of the Sixth Wisconsin Infantry, 1865.

Not waiting upon the Washington bureaucracy, the state legislature had meanwhile adopted a bill on April 15, 1864 that permitted veteran regiments and other Wisconsin units to receive new colors. Under this legislation, new colors were provided in 1864 to four veteran and nine non-veteran regiments.[114] The same legislation allowed the state quartermaster general to furnish colors to six other Wisconsin regiments in 1865, three of which had "veteranized" (re-enlisted) in 1864.[115] Among these was the Sixth Wisconsin Veteran Infantry, which, with the Seventh Wisconsin Veteran Infantry, continued the traditions of the old Iron Brigade after the final reorganization of February, 1865.

---

[113]A.W. Randall to Secretary of War Edwin M. Stanton, October 3, 1864; response of October 27, 1864; endorsements and enclosures, in Consolidated Correspondence File of the Quartermaster General, 1794–1914 (Record Group 92), subject heading "Flags," National Archives.

[114]*Acts of a General Nature Passed by the Legislature of Wisconsin in the Year 1864, Together with Joint Resolutions and Memorials* (Madison, 1864), 319–320. For the legislative history of this law, see *Journal of the Proceedings of the Senate...1864*, pp. 100, 360, 367, 368, 374, 504–505, 589, 591, 598, and 648, as well as *Journal of the Proceedings of the Assembly of Wisconsin during the Session for the Year 1864* (Madison, 1864), 527, 536, 537, 550, 551, 658, 673, and 767.

[115]Wis. QMG, Letter Books, Vol. 4, pp. 501, 505–506, 510–511, 516–520, 536, 538, 550–552, 553–554, 557, 561, 563–564, 569–570, 581–582, 583, 594–595, 596, 597, 598, 619, 622, 623, 644, 665, 672, 674, 675–676, 681, 683, 687–688. See also *Annual Report of the Quartermaster General...1864*, p. 421, and *Annual Report of the Quartermaster General of the State of Wisconsin for the Fiscal Year Ending September 30, 1865* (Madison, 1866), 1213.

The order for the new national color for the Sixth Wisconsin was drafted just before active campaigning began in the East in the spring of 1865. On March 24, the Wisconsin quartermaster general, J.M. Lynch, placed the order for this flag with Gilbert Hubbard & Co.:[116]

> By order of the Governor, you are hereby requested to make for this State, one Stand of National Regimental Colors for the 6th Reg't Wisconsin Vet. Vol. Inf'y, to be also inscribed as follows, with the names of battles in which the regiment had been engaged, viz: Gainesville, Bull Run, South Mountain, Antietam, Fredericksburg, Fitz Hugh's Crossing, Chancellorsville, Gettysburg, Mine Run, Wilderness, Spottsylvania, Laurel Hill, North Anna, Cold Harbor, Petersburg, Weldon Railroad, 1st Hatcher's Run, 2d Hatcher's Run. Please forward the flag to me, by American Express, as soon as completed.

The resulting color reflected a major deviation from the national colors Gilbert Hubbard & Co. had provided Wisconsin during 1864. Like most of the national colors made since late 1863, the unit's name was abbreviated on the center stripe in gold block letters (shadowed black, low and left): "6ᵀᴴ REGᵀ WIS. VET. VOL. INFANTRY." The full listing of battle honors, agreeable with Lynch's order, was painted in shadowed gold block letters on the two red stripes below the canton, each stripe containing two horizontal rows of honors across its full length. The canton, however, differed from the 1864 issues in that the thirty-five gold stars were arranged in seven horizontal rows of five stars each instead of the six staggered rows that typified the 1864 issues.[117]

---

[116]Wis. QMG, Letter Books, Vol. 4, pp. 675–676.

[117]This color measures seventy-two and a half inches on the staff by seventy-one inches on the fly, not including the two-and-a-quarter-inch-deep yellow silk fringe. The unit designation is painted in two-and-a-half-inch-high letters, reading properly on the obverse, but painted in reverse on the other side. The canton measures thirty-nine inches on the staff by twenty-six inches on the fly, and its gold stars are one and three-quarters inches across their points, inclusive of the alternating black and yellow highlights. As with all the later colors produced by Gilbert Hubbard & Co., the flag was secured to its staff by means of a sleeve lined in linen and two and a quarter inches in diameter formed by doubling over the leading edge of the flag. During 1864, the usual star pattern on Gilbert Hubbard & Co. flags furnished on contract to Wisconsin had been six horizontal rows of stars, arranged either 6,5,6,6,6,6, or 6,6,6,6,5,6 stars per row.

By the time this color was completed, the remnants of the old Iron Brigade had fought their last campaign. Two days after Lee's army had surrendered to Grant near the small hamlet of Appomattox Court House, Virginia, the Wisconsin quartermaster general forwarded the veteran Sixth's new national color to Lieutenant Colonel Thomas Kerr.[118] The new color would lead the regiment on its triumphant march through Washington during the Grand Review of the Army of the Potomac in May. Immediately behind, in stark contrast, followed the battle-worn national color of the veteran Seventh. From Washington, the flags of the veteran Sixth and the veteran Seventh would travel to Louisville, Kentucky, and at last, in July, back to Madison. There the flags were formally returned to the state, rejoining the colors that had been sent home in 1863 and 1864.

Never again would the flags of the Iron Brigade fly above the smoke and din of combat. Like the veterans who had borne them, they had returned home in glory, to be honored and then honorably retired. But their day was far from over. Even before the Civil War ended, the flags had been propelled into the political arena, and now they were to begin a new career as symbols and artifacts of the triumphant Union.

---

[118]Wis. QMG, Letter Books, Vol. 4, p. 678.

*Regimental
state color
of the
Second
Wisconsin
Infantry,
1863–1864:
one of the
first of two
state flags
authorized
by the
Wisconsin
legislature.*

*Regimental
state color
of the
Second
Wisconsin
Infantry,
1861–1863
(obverse).*

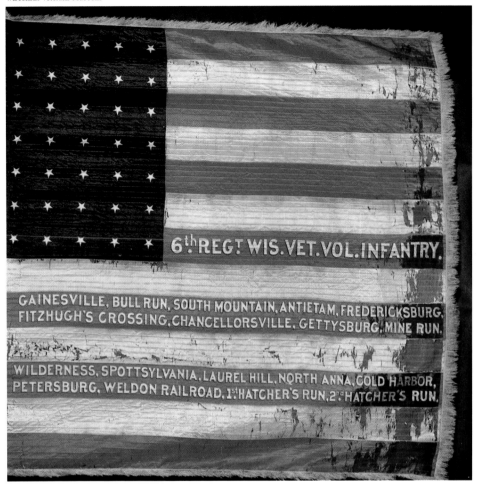

National flag of the Sixth Wisconsin Infantry. This color was the last one issued to the regiment and probably never saw combat. It did participate in the Grand Review and in the Bloody Shirt era following the war.

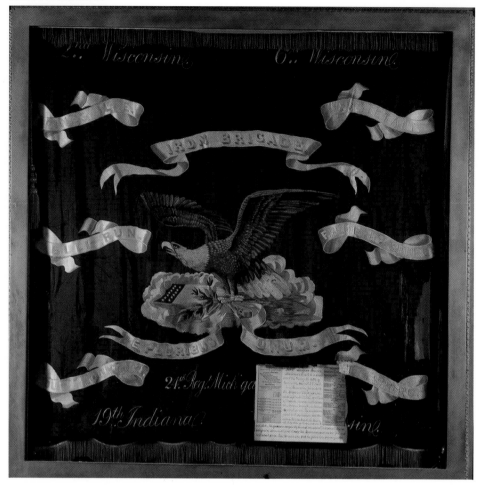

***Iron Brigade
presentation flag
manufactured by
Tiffany & Co.,
presented in
1863.***

Part II

Beyond the Battle

Beyond the Battle:
The Flags of the Iron Brigade, 1863–1918

By Richard H. Zeitlin

State officials, politicians, military figures, and charitable workers recognized the importance of the Iron Brigade's Civil War
flags, as well as those of other state units, well before the conflict ended in 1865. Some people believed that the battle flags
symbolized the Union cause: artifacts to be forever associated
with the sacrifices required to maintain national unity. After the
war, politicians used the banners to advertise themselves during
electoral campaigns. Legislators passed acts ostensibly to preserve them. Veterans rallied behind their tattered folds. Museums were created to house them. The flags became relics,
emblematic of state and national pride.

The Civil War battle flags played an important part in the main-
tenance of state cultural and political traditions, particularly during the lifetime of the generation that had experienced the Civil
War. Even today, 132 years after those momentous events, the
flags evoke an emotional response from those who view them.

Between 1863 and 1918, the flags participated in a variety of
significant events. Before 1865, the flags were used to encourage charitable donations for sick and wounded soldiers as well
as to promote enlistments into the army. Between 1866 and
1870, Wisconsin's Radical Republican politicians used the flags
to dramatize the Reconstruction issue, to blame the South as
well as the Democratic party for starting the war, and to organize state veterans into their political camp. The flags became
associated with the ebb and flow of what became known na-
tionally as "Waving the Bloody Shirt" politics by stimulating war-
time memories. They were featured at mass gatherings and rallies
during the nation's Centennial celebration in 1876. The Civil

Waukesha Historical Society

Waukesha Home Guards (later Company F, Fifth Wisconsin Infantry) in gray state militia uniforms, 1861. Companies of the Second and Seventh Wisconsin Infantry were issued similar uniforms.

War flags helped attract thousands of Wisconsin veterans into the ranks of regimental associations and into military fraternities such as the Grand Army of the Republic (GAR), especially after 1880. Once organized, the veterans successfully lobbied Congress for the adoption of pension legislation on behalf of Union soldiers which cost the federal treasury hundreds of millions of dollars after 1890. It is little wonder that citizens of Wisconsin took an interest in the status of state Civil War flags.

Selected flags of Wisconsin Iron Brigade regiments first began appearing at public events in 1863 when the United States Sanitary Commission, a national relief agency, used them as part of a fund-raising fair in Chicago. Sanitary Commission volunteers contributed to the war effort by caring for sick and wounded soldiers. As the war dragged on, caring for the injured became an even larger responsibility and one which required considerable sums of money.[1]

Mrs. Mary Livermore and Mrs. A.H. Hoge, both of Chicago, developed what became the Sanitary Commission's most impor-

---

[1]Dr. J.S. Newberry, *The U.S. Sanitary Commission in the Valley of the Mississippi During the War of the Rebellion, 1861–1865. Final Report of Dr. J.S. Newberry, Secretary Western Department* (Cleveland, 1871), 112–113; Ethel A. Hurn, *Wisconsin Women in the War* (Madison, 1911), 49.

tant mechanism for raising war relief funds, the "sanitary fair."[2] Hoge and Livermore originated the idea of the sanitary fair, which functioned by offering donated produce for sale as well as the wares of manufacturers and salesmen. As an attracting feature, exhibits of historical artifacts and war trophies—or curiosities—went on view.[3]

Hoge and Livermore organized the nation's first sanitary fair. Popularly named the "Woman's Fair" or the "Pioneer Fair," the Northwestern Sanitary Fair opened in Chicago on October 28, 1863. After paying fifty cents admission, visitors could view a selection of war trophies on display at the Cook County Court House. Mrs. E.H. Carr of Madison brought the battle flags of six Wisconsin units, including the Iron Brigade's Second and Sixth Wisconsin regiments, which were displayed on the east wall of the courthouse.[4]

Thousands visited the displays, and the fair netted $86,000 in two weeks. "More attractive than aught else," reported an observer, "were the battle torn flags. . . . A heartfelt and tearful interest clustered around them: and though rent in shreds, discolored, soiled, and blood stained, they lent a lustre to the walls. . . ."[5] "Noble witnesses of the valor of Wisconsin's brave sons" is how a *Milwaukee Sentinel* reporter described the state's regimental banners.[6]

The Chicago sanitary fair touched off a series of fairs throughout the country. Three other fairs took place in the Old Northwest, and Iron Brigade battle flags were present at all of them.[7]

The first of these took place at Quincy, Illinois.[8] Among the historical attractions were ten "old flags" from various Wisconsin regiments. State Quartermaster General Nathaniel F. Lund included a regimental banner from the Iron Brigade's Sixth Wis-

---

[2]Mrs. A.H. Hoge, *The Boys in Blue; or, Heroes of the Rank and File* (New York, 1867), 333–335; L.P. Brockett and Mrs. M.C. Vaughn, *Women's Work in the Civil War* (Philadelphia, 1867), 560–561; Rev. E.P. Smith, *Incidents of the U.S. Christian Commision* (New York, 1868), *passim*; Frank Moore, *Women of the War, Their Heroism and Self Sacrifice* (Hartford, Connecticut, 1866), 581–582, 592.

[3]Hoge, *ibid.*, p.7; Brockett and Vaughn, *Women's Work*, 575.

[4]*History of the Northwestern Soldiers Fair Held in Chicago the Last Week of October and the First Week of November, 1863; Including a List of Donations and Names of Donors* (Chicago, 1864), 29; *Milwaukee Sentinel*, October 30, 1863.

[5]Hoge, *Boys in Blue*, 340; *History of the Northwestern Soldiers Fair*, 29.

[6]*Milwaukee Sentinel*, November 14, 1863.

[7]Hoge, *Boys in Blue*, 333.

[8]*History of the Northwestern Soldiers Fair*, 29.

WHi (x3) 12866

WHi (x3) 45244

6th Wis Colors Iron Brigade

Torn and tattered, the national color of the Second Wisconsin was posed by a photographer at one of the 1863 sanitary fairs held in Illinois.

After its return to Wisconsin in 1863, the 1861 issue national color of the Sixth Wisconsin was sent to at least four sanitary fairs to assist in fund raising for the Sanitary Commission.

consin and the national colors of the Seventh Wisconsin in the group he sent to Quincy in October, 1864. Lund advised fair organizers of the importance of the artifacts, observing, "these colors are kept by the State of Wisconsin as sacredly as a trust committed to her by her sons who have suffered for the life of the nation."[9]

Six months later, the flags were again dispatched to Illinois. This time nearly all of the colors of the Iron Brigade, forty-three flags of additional Wisconsin regiments, ten captured Confederate flags, and assorted prizes of war appeared at the second or Great Northwest Sanitary Fair which opened in Chicago in May, 1865.[10] Wisconsin State Quartermaster General James M. Lynch

[9] N.F. Lund to Mrs. A.S. Morton, October 2, 3, 1864, Wisconsin National Guard, Quartermaster Corps, Outgoing Correspondence, Letter Books, 1861–1873, Wisconsin State Archives, State Historical Society of Wisconsin. Cited hereinafter as Wis. QMG with type of document and date.

[10] N.F. Lund to Mrs. A.S. Morton, October 27, 1864; James M. Lynch to James B. Bradwell, May 1, 1865; both in Wis. QMG Letter Books.

reminded Chicago fair organizers that Wisconsin's battle flags "have a value to the people of this state which cannot be estimated," and he urged that the "utmost care" be taken to prevent damaging the "relic" flags.[11] The Great Fair was immensely successful. General William T. Sherman visited the fair, as did thousands of soldiers and other citizens. The fair netted $270,000 in four weeks.[12]

As soon as the Great Northwest Sanitary Fair ended, the flags and other war trophies were taken to Milwaukee, to be displayed at the Soldiers Home Fair.[13] In the rush to ship the trophies to Milwaukee, however, a Confederate flag captured by Wisconsin troops at Vicksburg was lost. Quartermaster General Lynch expressed "deep grief" over the loss, explaining to fair authorities that "the trophies possess a peculiar value, which cannot be estimated in money. . . ."[14] State officials never recovered the lost banner.[15]

The Soldiers Home Fair was the largest charitable effort undertaken by Wisconsin's citizens during the Civil War era. Mrs. Lydia Hewitt and Mrs. Henrietta Colt of Milwaukee helped provide leadership and direction for the event. State legislators appropriated $5,000 towards the purchase of the federal military hospital in Milwaukee and for transforming the West Water Street building into an asylum for disabled veterans. Proceeds of the Soldiers Home Fair provided funds for the construction of a new soldiers' home in the Milwaukee suburb of Wauwatosa.[16]

The Soldiers Home Fair opened on June 28, 1865, in a specially constructed building located on the corner of Huron Street and

---

[11]*Ibid.*, J.M. Lynch to J.B. Bradwell, May 22, 1865; J.M. Lynch to J.B. Bradwell, May 20, 1865; both in Wis. QMG Letter Books.

[12]*Wisconsin State Journal* (Madison), June 22, 1865; *Chicago Tribune*, June 2, 1865.

[13]J.M. Lynch to J.B. Bradwell, May 15, 1865; J.M. Lynch to E.S. Buttrick, May 24, 1865; both in Wis. QMG Letter Books.

[14]J.M. Lynch to J.B. Bradwell, June 22, 1865, *ibid.*

[15]*Annual Reports of the Adjutant General and the Quartermaster General of the State of Wisconsin, 1865* (Madison, 1865), 1216. Cited hereinafter as *Rpt. Wis. Adj. Gen.* and *Rpt. Wis. QMG* by date.

[16]Hurn, *Wisconsin Women*, 167–173; Frank Klement, "Wisconsin and the Civil War," *Wisconsin Blue Book, 1962* p.177; J.M. Lynch to William Allen, June 17, 1865, Wis. QMG Letter Books; Proclamation of Governor James T. Lewis, *Home Fair Journal*, May 20, 1865.

A close-up of some soldiers on Main Street during the 1865 Soldiers Home Fair Parade in Milwaukee.

West Broadway.[17] The war had been over for just two months. "A long night of gloom had passed away," observed an Iron Brigade veteran who attended the carnival-like event. "No pencil can adequately describe the joy. . . ."[18]

Fair organizers netted $100,183.88. Additional contributions raised the amount by nearly $10,000. The fifty-five Wisconsin battle flags were returned to Madison in July, after the Soldiers Home Fair ended its two-week run.[19] The battle flags had demonstrated their widespread appeal, not only to veterans and their supporters but to the general public as well.

While sanitary fair volunteers had used Iron Brigade and other unit flags to stimulate attendance, recruiters had been using them to fill the army's depleted ranks by encouraging enlistments prior to the war's end. In January, 1864, for example, Brigadier General Edward S. Bragg of Fond du Lac, who had risen from a captaincy to command of the Iron Brigade, led the furloughed veterans of the Sixth Wisconsin through the streets of Milwau-

---

[17]Hurn, *Wisconsin Women; Home Fair Journal,* June 29, 1865.

[18]"At the Opening of the Fair," box 2, Jerome A. Watrous Papers, Wisconsin State Archives.

[19] *Wisconsin State Journal,* July 13, September 8, 1865; James M. Lynch to William Allen, July 31, 1865, Wis. QMG Letter Books; *Rpt. Wis. QMG, 1865,* p.1216.

The procession of the soldiers during the 1865 parade.

kee to a reception city officials arranged in their honor. Bragg and Brigadier General Lucius Fairchild of Madison, who was still recovering from the loss of his left arm at Gettysburg and was now secretary of state under the administration of Governor James T. Lewis, harangued Milwaukeeans who flocked to

Women participating in the Soldiers Home Fair Parade.

the Chamber of Commerce building to witness the event, challenging young men to volunteer for war service. Fairchild brought one of the flags of the Sixth Infantry with him from Madison. "Continuous cheers" greeted the veterans and their flag, reported Frank A. Flower, a historian and political ally of Fairchild present at the occasion.[20]

Lucius Fairchild appreciated the emotional power of the battle flags. His own association with the Iron Brigade's Second Wisconsin Infantry had left the one-armed, aspiring politician with a keen interest in the public appearances made by the Iron Brigade flags. Fairchild stood under the flags of the Second Wisconsin in Madison in June of 1864, for instance, when the command returned home to muster out. Fairchild had the regiment's old banners displayed in the park surrounding the state capitol while he reminded the veterans of their duty to become virtuous citizens by taking an interest in political affairs.[21] It had also been Fairchild who assembled the flags and other artifacts to be exhibited at the Chicago Sanitary Fair and the Soldiers Home Fair, where those of the Iron Brigade were so conspicuously represented.[22]

Wisconsin began dismantling its military apparatus after the Confederacy surrendered in April, 1865. Returning soldiers deposited thousands of muskets, numerous artillery pieces with related equipment, tents, camp gear, ammunition, and other accouterments with officials in Madison. No armory building existed. The amount of war material overwhelmed the storage capacity of the state, and arms and equipment "are scattered all about the Capitol building and park," reported the state quartermaster general.[23] Some people expressed concern over public safety because of the haphazardly stored war supplies.[24]

Wisconsin officials naturally sought to acquire the banners of the returning regiments. Efforts were made to collect, catalog,

[20]Frank A. Flower, *History of Milwaukee from Pre-historic Times to the Present Day* (2 vols., Chicago, 1881), 1:728.

[21]*Wisconsin State Journal*, June 15, 18, 20, 21, 1864; Sam Ross, *The Empty Sleeve: A Biography of Lucius Fairchild* (Madison, 1964), 63.

[22]F.J. Blair to Lucius Fairchild, June 23, 1865; William Allen to Fairchild, June 30, 1865; both in the Lucius Fairchild Papers, Wisconsin State Archives. George H. Otis, *The Second Wisconsin Infantry,* edited by Alan D. Gaff (Dayton, 1984), 7–21.

[23]*Rpt. Wis. QMG, 1867,* p. 441. There was no Quartermaster General's Report in 1866, The report of 1867, therefore, contains a two-year summary.

[24]*Rpt. Wis. Adj. Gen.,* 1867, p. 6.

and protect them. During the war, state lawmakers had required regimental officers to turn over their war-torn banners before receiving new sets of replacement colors. This process, largely accomplished in 1864, left the state in possession of forty-nine national, thirty-nine regimental, and sixteen smaller flags and guidons.[25] The quartermaster general's office took charge of the "honorable rags," repairing some of the damage occasioned by battles and field use.[26] "They have been put in the best possible condition that could be devised for their preservation," reported Quartermaster General Lund in October, 1864. He went on to mention the fact that hundreds of citizens had visited his office to see the flags, "the noblest record that can exist, of the bravery of her [Wisconsin's] sons."[27]

After the millions of men in the Union Army had finally mustered out, certain regimental flags were to have been sent to Washington for federal safekeeping. Governor James T. Lewis, however, requested permission from the War Department authorizing Wisconsin to keep all the flags of its own regiments. Lund explained, ". . .the possession of these colors is very desirable in order to complete the collection of flags borne during the war by Wisconsin regiments."[28] Washington agreed, and the state quartermaster general's office catalogued the regimental colors along with a record of the engagements in which each unit had participated. Lund then had the flags "thoroughly repaired" and stored in a "mixed pile" in the basement of the capitol.[29]

Governor Lewis, Adjutant General Augustus Gaylord, and Quartermaster Generals Lund and Lynch had acquired title to 195 state battle flags. Repairs had been carried out. Public exhibitions had demonstrated the interest that some citizens had for

---

[25]*Rpt. Wis. QMG, 1865*, p. 1214; *Acts of a General Nature Passed by the Legislature in 1864 Together With Resolutions and Memorials* (Madison, 1864), Chap. 248, Sec. 2. Cited hereinafter as *Laws of Wisconsin* by year.

[26]*Ibid.; Rpt. Wis. QMG, 1864*, p. 423.

[27]*Ibid.*

[28]*Ibid., 1865*, p. 1214; J.M. Lynch to John H. Brown, October 19, 1865, Wis. QMG Letter Books; "List of Regimental Colors, Which Have Been Borne by Wisconsin Volunteer Regiments During the Rebellion and Memoranda of the Battles in Which They Have Been Carried," no date, *ibid.*, vol. 4, pp. 691–697; J.M. Lynch to Col. Charles S. Love, August 3, 1865, *ibid.*

[29]J.M. Lynch to Lt. Col. G.R. Giddings, August 22, 1865; Lynch to Giddings, September 19, 1865; Lynch to Giddings, November 20, 1865; S. Nye Gibbs to Lt. Col. C. Hobbs, February 19, 1866; all in Wis. QMG Letter Books. See also *Rpt. Wis. QMG, 1865*, pp. 1003–1004; and *Rpt. Wis. Adj. Gen., 1867*, p. 442.

the banners. Visitors to the quartermaster general's office, many of whom were ex-soldiers, reinforced the belief that the flags had unique significance. "Proper exhibition," Adjutant General Gaylord therefore concluded, "is a duty which we owe. . .to the gratification of the living and the memory of the dead."[30] Lynch echoed Gaylord's sentiments concerning the desirability of some form of display.[31]

More important than military supplies and battle flags, the end of the war had reintroduced over 70,000 veterans into the social, economic, and political life of Wisconsin. The total number of votes cast by Wisconsinites in 1864, a presidential year, amounted to 149,342. If they chose to exercise their franchise, veterans represented a sizable portion of Wisconsin's electorate.[32]

The ex-soldiers faced important adjustment problems when they returned home. The number of wounded men has never even been officially counted. As with wounds, sickness contracted in the South continued to kill or incapacitate. Limbless, blind, injured, diseased, and otherwise handicapped soldiers returned to a society where social service agencies hardly existed. The widows and orphans of soldiers were especially hard-pressed. Jobs, trades, and farms had been taken over by others during the war, leaving the task of re-entering the economy to the veterans' own resources. Considering the size of the veteran population, the war experiences they had shared, and the readjustment challenges they faced, it is not surprising that politicians eagerly sought to become the soldier's friend. Bounty equalizations, pensions for those obviously disabled by wounds and disease, benefits for widows and dependents, creation of a state-supported soldiers' orphans home, and preferential consideration

---

[30] *Rpt. Wis. Adj. Gen., 1865,* pp. 730–731.

[31] *Ibid.,* pp. 1220–1221.

[32] *Ibid.,* pp. 20–21. Wisconsin was credited with providing 91,379 soldiers during 1861–1865. Of that number, 12,301 died from all causes; 5,782 men re-enlisted and were, therefore, counted twice. Thus, 73,296 Wisconsinites survived the war (a mortality rate of approximately 14 per cent). See William F. Fox, *Regimental Losses in the American Civil War* (New York, 1889), 526; Charles H. Estabrook, ed., *Wisconsin Losses in the Civil War; A List of the Names of Wisconsin Soldiers Killed in Action, Mortally Wounded, or Dying from other Causes in the Civil War* (Madison, 1915), *passim;* Wisconsin Adjutant General's Office, *Roster of Wisconsin Volunteers in the War of the Rebellion* (2 vols., Madison, 1886), *passim;* Charles R. Tuttle, *Illustrated History of Wisconsin* (Madison, 1875), 609, 618; "Wisconsin Vote in Presidential Elections, 1848–1980," *Wisconsin Blue Book, 1981,* p. 702.

for government jobs became issues in which veterans took a keen interest.

When Lucius Fairchild took office as governor in January, 1866, the level of political activities associated with veterans' affairs increased. Fairchild and his associates helped to organize Civil War veterans, encouraging them to vote as a bloc, and especially to tie their futures to the Republican party.

Fairchild used the Civil War battle flags to further his career. They became advertising devices in emotional anti-Southern, anti-Democratic political activities—Bloody Shirt campaigns— through which Fairchild and his supporters attained and kept themselves in office. A dynamic and impassioned speaker, the thirty-four-year-old Fairchild became a regionally important politician, the first of Wisconsin's seven soldier-governors, a national force within veterans' circles, and the state's first chief executive to be elected to three terms. While railroad, lumber, and commercial interests undoubtedly dominated Wisconsin politics in the thirty years following the war, some citizens and a number of politicians preoccupied themselves with Civil War themes.[33] Rather than confront potentially divisive questions such as those engendered by immigration, industrialization, monopolization, the concentration of wealth, urbanization, and labor unrest, Fairchild and his supporters (and even some of his rivals) remained complacently identified with issues stemming out of the Civil War. Sharp partisanship, of course, remained a feature of postwar state politics, and such controversial matters as federal subsidies for internal improvements, prohibition, inflationary paper money, as well as regulating railroads and the mandatory use of English in public schools certainly affected the battles for office between Republicans and Democrats. But the desire on the part of leading members of both major political parties in Wisconsin (and throughout the North) to please the approximately 2,500,000 Union veterans and potential voters had important consequences at all levels of government. To be sure, the effective organizing of the veterans did not occur overnight. Nearly twenty years passed before the ex-soldiers were welded into a truly recognizable unified national pressure group. Organizing took place in fits and starts, and initial successes during the period 1865–1869 were followed by a decade of failures.

---

[33]Robert C. Nesbit, *Wisconsin: A History* (Madison, 1973), 303, 314–320, 362–373, 381.

Early in 1866 Fairchild helped organize the Wisconsin chapter of the Soldiers' and Sailors' National Union League, an association formed by eastern veterans.[34] Local Union League members included such Fairchild allies as Jeremiah M. Rusk, a farmer and businessman from Viroqua, ex-colonel of the Twenty-fifth Wisconsin Infantry, state bank comptroller, and a political office seeker; Thomas S. Allen, secretary of state, editor of the *Oshkosh Northwestern*, and Iron Brigade officer in Fairchild's Second Wisconsin who had been wounded at Antietam; James A. Kellogg, last colonel of the Sixth Wisconsin, now a Wausau attorney; and James K. Proudfit of Madison, colonel of the Twelfth Wisconsin and now state adjutant general, who became Union League president. Cassius Fairchild, the governor's brother who had been wounded at Shiloh, became vice-president.[35] Nearly all Union League members from Wisconsin, as elsewhere, were active Republicans. The Union League lobbied for veterans' preference in jobs and aid for disabled soldiers. But the organization quickly affiliated itself with Radical Republicans in Congress and joined their efforts to thwart President Andrew Johnson's Reconstruction program for the defeated Confederate states.[36] Wisconsin's Union League members became, with few exceptions, a leadership cadre of Radical Republican veteran activists who helped to form and promote another military society with a broadly based western membership: the Grand Army of the Republic.

Between February and May of 1866, Fairchild initiated contact with Illinois soldier-politicians who had founded the GAR and who were associated with John A. Logan, ex-commander of the XV Corps, a leading congressional Radical, and soon to be National GAR Commander.[37] James K. Proudfit became Wisconsin's

---

[34]Mary R. Dearing, *Veterans in Politics: The Story of the G.A.R.* (Baton Rouge, 1952), 69.

[35]Soldiers' and Sailors' National Union League, Accounts of Members, General Records, 1866–1880, in the Archives, Wisconsin Veterans Museum, Madison; Ross, *Empty Sleeve*, 82–99; Henry Casson, *"Uncle Jerry," The Life of Jeremiah M. Rusk* (Madison, 1895), 156–157; Grand Army Publishing Company, *Soldiers' and Citizens' Album* (2 vols., Chicago, 1891), 2:695–699; Tuttle, *Wisconsin*, 598; Robert B. Beath, *History of the Grand Army of the Republic with Introduction by Lucius Fairchild* (New York, 1888), 543.

[36]Dearing, *Veterans in Politics*.

[37]*Ibid.*, 94; *Wisconsin State Journal*, February 26, May 26, 1866; George F. Dawson, *Life and Service of Gen. John A. Logan* (New York, 1888), 123–125; Mary H. Stephenson, *Dr. B.F. Stephenson, Founder of the Grand Army of the Republic* (Springfield, Illinois, 1894), *passim*; Major Oliver M. Wilson, *The Grand Army of the Republic Under Its First Constitution: Its Birth and Organization* (Kansas City, 1905), *passim*.

commander as the Badger State organized the first GAR department outside Illinois.[38] The GAR adopted the trappings of a
fraternal benevolent society with a secret initiation ritual.[39] In
1866 Fairchild helped recruit eastern veterans—who had been
attracted to Soldiers' and Sailors' Union Leagues and similar organizations—to the GAR during a massive veterans' rally held in
Pittsburgh to support congressional Republican Radicals.[40]

In July, 1866, Fairchild organized an elaborate ceremony in
Madison to commemorate the end of the war and to show off
the strength and popularity of the soldier element. Battle flags
and veterans were prominently featured. On July 4, contingents
of veterans from each Wisconsin regiment were assembled at
the state capitol, and they selected a color-guard to carry the
unit's banners. The flags would be formally presented to the
state by the men who bore them during the war. Fairchild invited military figures and guests from across the nation.[41]

Officials of local units of government as well as Wisconsin congressmen and senators attended the Madison gathering. Some
20,000 people flocked to Wisconsin's capital city on the appointed day, clogging local roads while tripling the population
of the city.[42] Rain showers let up and the Fourth of July dawned
clear, cool, and beautiful. Madisonians draped flags from their

[38]Beath, *Grand Army of the Republic*, 537–539; *Soldiers and Citizens Album*, 2:768.
[39]Wisconsin G.A.R., *Proceedings of the First Annual Encampment by Department of Wisconsin* (Madison, 1867). Also see J. Worth Carnahan, *Manual of the Civil War and Key to the Grand Army of the Republic and Kindred Societies* (Chicago, 1897), 18–25; and Beath, *Grand Army of the Republic*, 41–43.
[40]Beath, *ibid.*, 26–31; Fairchild to Soldiers and Sailors Convention, September 23, 1866, in the Fairchild Papers; Governor Hacheld to Fairchild, September 12, 1866, *ibid.*; Dearing, *Veterans in Politics*, 98; George Lankevitch, "The G.A.R. in New York State, 1865–1898" (doctoral dissertation, Columbia University, 1967), 53–55; Wilson, *The Grand Army of the Republic Under Its First Constitution*, 192.
[41]L.A. Dayton to Lucius Fairchild, June 25, 1866; Adam Badeau to Fairchild, June 26, 1866; Paul Dillingham to Fairchild, June 6, 1866; J.D. Cox to Fairchild, June 6, 1866; Alex Bullock to Fairchild, June 19, 1866; Robert A. McCoy to Farichild, June 8, 1866; Thomas Swan to Fairchild, June 14, 1866; Samuel Cory to Fairchild, June 7, 1866; Gen M.F. Force to Fairchild, June 12, 1866; William Dennison to Fairchild, June 14, 1866; Henry Dodge to Fairchild, June 15, 1866; all in Department of Executive, Administration, Military Correspondence, 1844–1910, box 2, Wisconsin State Archives. Cited hereinafter as Gov. Military Corr.
[42]Henry Palmer to Fairchild, June 27, 1866; William T. Henry to Fairchild, June 5, 1866; John J. Tallmadge to Fairchild, June 12, 1866; Charles N. Eldridge to Fairchild, June 20, 1866; Senator Timothy O. Howe to Fairchild, June 29, 1866; Charles N. Schaeffer to Fairchild, June 7, 1866; Thomas Swan to Fairchild, June 14, 1866; all in Gov. Military Corr. See also John Robertson, *The Flags of Michigan*, (Lansing, 1877), 82; and Daniel S. Durrie, *A History of Madison, the Capitol of Wisconsin* (Madison, 1874), 311.

homes while church bells pealed and cannon salutes sounded. It was "a day that will ever be remembered in the history of Madison," noted a *Wisconsin State Journal* reporter.[43] The parade moved down State Street to Gilman, then southward along Pinckney and east on Wilson Street before returning to the Capitol Park. Bands from Madison, Oregon, and Beaver Dam blared while citizens and guests fell in behind the detachment of veterans carrying the regimental colors, led by the flags of the "glorious Iron Brigade."[44] "There was one feature in the procession which riveted the attention of all," noted a reporter. "It was the . . . battle flags . . . some torn until only a few shreds were left. . . ."[45]

Judge William P. Lyon, ex-colonel of the Thirteenth Infantry, delivered the formal speech presenting the flags to the state. "These banners are the. . .symbols of our national unity, the material representations of the institutions of freedom. . . ," the judge explained. "Hence do these banners become to us the symbols and emblems and mementos of all the labors and sacrifices. . .of the people. . . ."[46]

Governor Fairchild accepted the flags in the name of the state and delivered a ringing speech in which he promised the veterans that their flags would be installed at the capitol "as monuments of glory" for as "long as this government shall stand. . . ."[47] Fairchild went on to say that "a grateful people are not unmindful of the debt" owed the veterans, and "that a generous country will never count her whole duty done until both you and yours are raised above all danger of want."[48] The one-armed soldiers' friend devoted much of his remaining life to achieving that goal.

After the ceremony, the flags were taken to the capitol and "placed in different offices and in the rooms of the State Historical Society" in such a manner that they could be "seen but not handled."[49] Fairchild had become friendly with Lyman C. Draper,

[43] *Wisconsin State Journal,* July 5, 1866.
[44] *Ibid.*
[45] *Ibid.*
[46] "Speech of William P. Lyon, July 4, 1866," in the Hosea W. Rood Papers, Archives, Wisconsin Veterans Museum.
[47] "Address Delivered July 4, 1866 upon the Formal Delivery of the Battle Flags to the State," in the Fairchild Papers.
[48] *Ibid.*
[49] *Rpt. Wis. Adj. Gen., 1867,* p. 442.

superintendent of the historical society, and the governor secured space in the Executive Department rooms in the capitol
to house the society's collections.[50]

In August, Fairchild joined Senator Timothy O. Howe; one-legged
Milwaukee soldier-politician, Congressman Halbert E. Paine; Jerry
Rusk; and ex-governor Edward Salomon for a series of pro-
Radical meetings denouncing Democrats and President Johnson.[51]
In Madison shortly thereafter, Wisconsin Radical Republicans
hung captured Confederate flags upside down "in token of sub-
jugation" while the governor harangued a crowd in the Assembly chambers.[52] Prior to the fall election, Governor Fairchild
allowed a group of Wisconsin battle flags to appear at a veterans' political gathering in Burlington. Fairchild requested that
Jacob S. Crane, organizer of the rally and a former officer of the
Forty-third Wisconsin, "send a careful man" to Madison to pick
up the flags: *They are too sacred to be entrusted to a common
carrier.*"[53]

To preserve the Union victory, won at such enormous cost,
Wisconsin's Radical politicians continually urged veterans
and other citizens to vote Republican.[54] Healthy Republican
majorities vindicated the Bloody Shirt campaign technique in
1866, although Democrats still retained a number of seats in the
Wisconsin Senate. In fact, throughout the period 1860–1890 the
Republican party could not take its victories for granted, either
on the state or national levels. Democrats remained electorally
competitive, possibly because of their strong base among some
ethnic groups and among Southerners.[55]

In 1867, for example, Fairchild was narrowly re-elected by a
majority of only 4,564 votes out of a total of over 140,000 cast.
The slim margin shocked the governor and convinced some

---

[50]Clifford Lord and Carl Ubbelohde, *Clio's Servant: The State Historical Society of Wisconsin, 1846–1954* (Madison, 1967), 42, 56–57, 64–65.
[51]*Wisconsin State Journal*, August 9, 1866.
[52]*Ibid.*, August 13, 1866.
[53]Fairchild to J.S. Crane, October 10, 1866, in the Fairchild Papers.
[54]Ross, *Empty Sleeve*, 93; Dearing, *Veterans in Politics*, 105, 111; Fairchild to T.O. Howe, July 24, 1866, in the Fairchild Papers.
[55]Nesbit, *Wisconsin*, 363–364; Ross, *Empty Sleeve*, 96. See also Edward Gambill, *Conservative Ordeal: Northern Democrats and Reconstruction, 1865–1869* (Ames, Iowa, 1981), *passim*; and Lankevitch, "G.A.R. in New York State," 53–55.

rival Republican factions to try to drop the Bloody Shirt technique as well as its most vociferous local practitioner at the next opportunity.[56] The meager victory threw Fairchild, on the other hand, into a frenzy of political activity during 1868. He played the veteran card to its maximum extent, earning a national reputation for himself in the process.

In May, 1868, Fairchild convened the meeting of the Wisconsin Soldiers' and Sailors' Association in Milwaukee. He secured from the soldiers their endorsement for the Republican party in the coming election and had himself selected to lead the state delegation to the National Soldiers' and Sailors' Convention scheduled to gather in Chicago at the same time that the Republican National Convention would be nominating a presidential candidate.[57] Fairchild, Proudfit, Rusk, and Judge W. H. Sessions, an ex-captain of the Twenty-first Wisconsin, carried a group of Wisconsin battle flags, including those of the Iron Brigade's Second Regiment, to Chicago.[58]

At the national soldiers' gathering, Fairchild was chosen as the presiding officer. Wisconsin's governor, in association with GAR Commander John Logan, convinced the assembled veterans to declare their "active support" of the Republican party as "the only political organization which . . . is true to the principles of loyalty, liberty, and equality before the law."[59] With the Republican party thus endorsed as the official veterans' party, conventioneers selected Ulysses S. Grant as the ex-soldiers' candidate for president.[60]

The veterans then held a parade, with Fairchild and the Wisconsin delegation following the tattered Civil War flags as they marched to the Crosby Opera House where the Republican convention was in full swing. Thousands of Chicago residents cheered the parading ex-soldiers and their flags. Fairchild informed the conventioneers of the veterans' preference. GAR Commander and Congressman Logan nominated Grant, whom

---

[56]Tuttle, *Wisconsin*, 609; Ross, *Empty Sleeve*, "Vote for Governor in General Elections, 1848–1978," *Wisconsin Blue Book, 1981*, p. 703.

[57]*Milwaukee Sentinel*, May 13, 1868.

[58]*Wisconsin State Journal*, May 20, 1868.

[59]"Platform of Principles Adopted by the Soldiers' and Sailors' National Convention at Chicago, May 19, 1868," in the Fairchild Papers; Frank A. Flower, *History of the Republican Party* (Springfield, Illinois, 1884), 293–294; *Milwaukee Sentinel*, May 20, 1868.

[60]*Milwaukee Sentinel*, May 20, 1868; Ross, *Empty Sleeve*, 97–98.

the delegates unanimously chose as the Republican candidate for president.[61]

Fairchild then formed Wisconsin Soldiers' Grant and Colfax Clubs. The governor toured Wisconsin rallying ex-soldiers and other citizens in support of Grant and his running-mate Schuyler Colfax. The Radicals missed no opportunity to equate the Democrats with civil war and treason. "Every rebel, every Copper head, every draft sneak, every dirty traitor," noted Governor Fairchild, would be voting for Democrats, as would members of the Ku Klux Klan.[62] The dividing line between the parties, explained the soldiers' friend at a veterans' gathering in Madison, "was drawn just about where it was during the war—between the loyal blue and the traitor gray."[63] Grant carried Wisconsin over-whelmingly. Fairchild then sought an unprecedented third term as governor, turning for support to the veterans as well as those interested in federal subsidies for internal improvements.

Fairchild received the support of soldier organizers like Jerry Rusk and S.W. Martin, editor of the *Soldier's Record*, a Madison newspaper geared to veterans. GAR meetings began to be held at the state capitol, and Governor Fairchild brought Iron Brigade flags to local GAR gatherings to stimulate attendance.[64] Among veterans, Fairchild's theme remained focused on Civil War animosities. The Democrats, in Fairchild's view, had "encouraged rebellion," supported the South, and, therefore, had "blood on their heads."[65] The governor won re-election by a healthy majority.[66]

Fairchild began his final term as governor by requesting that Wisconsin legislators authorize an expenditure to construct glass cases for the Civil War battle flags. He asked that the quartermaster general provide the cases "in order to preserve the valued relics."[67] Lyman Draper supported Fairchild's plea for

---

[61] *Ibid.*

[62] *Wisconsin State Journal*, May 25, July 22, 1868; Flower, *Republican Party*, 302–303; *Soldiers' and Citizens' Album*, 2:769; Beath, *Grand Army of the Republic*, 539–540; "Importance of the Election, 1868," in the Fairchild Papers.

[63] *Wisconsin State Journal*, August 5, 1868; Ross, *Empty Sleeve*, 101–102.

[64] Ross, *Empty Sleeve*, 122; Dearing, *Veterans in Politics*, 191–193; *Soldier's Record*, July 24, 1869; Casson, *"Uncle Jerry,"* 156–157; *Wisconsin State Journal*, February 6, 1869.

[65] Campaign Scrapbook, 1870, in the Fairchild Papers.

[66] Tuttle, *Wisconsin*, 618; *Wisconsin Blue Book, 1981*, p. 703.

[67] *Annual Messages of Wisconsin Governors*, 1870, p. 9.

"Wisconsin's Star Spangled Banners."[68] Legislators acted positively on the matter in March, 1870, passing an "act relating to the preservation of the colors and flags of our late regiments."[69]

The Milwaukee firm of Fisher and Reynolds constructed the cases, and the banners went on display in the State Historical Society's rooms in the capitol later that year.[70] A unique feature of the arrangement involved the fact that the historical society did not gain title to the Civil War banners. Rather, the flags remained under the control of the quartermaster general's office—an executive department. In Superintendent Draper's words, the flags had been "deposited with" the historical society.[71] Fairchild and his allies had scant interest in leaving the battle flags permanently in a museum. The arrangement with the historical society was not intended to interfere with the business of politics.

In September, for example, Fairchild, Paine, Proudfit, Rusk (by then state GAR commander), Judge Lyon, Senator Matthew H. Carpenter, and Governor Paul Austin of Minnesota attended the Wisconsin Soldiers' and Sailors' Reunion at the state fair in Milwaukee. Three thousand veterans attended the gathering at the "Rink," a fair building. Detachments of veterans paraded behind their regimental banners while onlookers cheered and politicians spoke. Members of several GAR posts attended the meeting. The central ornament above the speaker's podium was an Iron Brigade flag, and the entire state collection of flags "graced the sides and gallery of the auditorium."[72] Fairchild also permitted certain regimental banners to attend local reunions, such as those of Company K of the Eighth Wisconsin Infantry, organized by an ally of the governor.[73]

[68]Sixteenth Annual Report of the Executive Committee, 1870, *Collections of the State Historical Society of Wisconsin* (Madison, 1872), 30–31. Hereinafter cited as *SHSW Collections*.

[69]*Laws of Wisconsin, 1870,* Chap. 82.

[70]*Rpt. Wis. QMG, 1870,* p.78; Tuttle, *Wisconsin,* 614; Durrie, *Madison,* 319; Lord and Ubbelohde, *Clio's Servant,* 55–56.

[71]Sixteenth Annual Report, 1870, *SHSW Collections,* 31; Seventeenth Annual Report of the Executive Committee, 1872, *ibid.,* 53; *Rpt. Wis. QMG, 1871,* p. 30; *Laws of Wisconsin, 1870,* Chap. 82, Sec.1.

[72]*Milwaukee Sentinel,* September 27, 28, 29, 30, 1870; Beath, *Grand Army of the Republic,* 539.

[73]Reunion Book, Company "K", August 31, 1871, in the Augustus G. Weissert Papers, 1861–1923, Archives, Wisconsin Veterans Museum; *Soldier's Record,* October 16, 1869.

Throughout Fairchild's tenure as governor, Bloody Shirt campaign oratory proved to be an effective vote-getter, though it
was never the only technique in that capable soldier's political
repertoire. By the 1870's, however, Civil War issues appeared to
be somewhat less immediate than they had been during the
hectic 1865–1869 period. With Grant in the White House, Reconstruction seemed fairly settled, save for the rise of the Ku
Klux Klan in the South. The initial interest shown by Union
veterans in joining various soldiers' clubs and organizations like
the GAR slackened as the "boys," who were still young men,
devoted their efforts to raising families and earning a living. In
fact, some veterans believed (correctly) that the GAR was not an
independent soldiers' fraternity at all, but rather an instrument
of the Republican party which had accomplished relatively little
in securing jobs for non-officers, in pressuring for generous
bounty equalizations, or in liberalizing the existing invalid pension law of 1862. In addition, the GAR was hampered by a
"graded" system of membership, whereby rank distinctions existed among the initiates. Other problems which emerged to
plague the GAR in Wisconsin and across the North included
poor administration, lack of membership records, inadequate
dues collection, and general demoralization.[74] As State Commander Proudfit reported, the condition of the order was char-
acterized by "a chapter of irregularities and blunders that has no
parallel short of Shakespeare's comedy of errors."[75]

The voting populace had begun to show apathy towards Civil
War enmities in Wisconsin as the new decade dawned. Fairchild
sought a foreign appointment after the Republicans selected ex-
Major General Cadwallader C. Washburn of La Crosse as the
party's gubernatorial candidate. A Washburn rally, billed as a
soldiers' reunion, took place in La Crosse during early June,
1871. Fairchild sent twenty-two Wisconsin Civil War battle flags,
including a stand from each Iron Brigade regiment. But only

---

[74]Dearing, *Veterans in Politics,* 187, 209–211, 213; Frank H. Heck, *The Civil
War Veteran In Minnesota Life and Politics* (Oxford, Ohio, 1941), 203; Beath,
Grand Army of the Republic, 31–32, 539; Hosea W. Rood, "The Grand Army of the
Republic and the Department of Wisconsin: Origin of the G.A.R.," in the *Wisconsin
Magazine of History,* 6: 282, 287–288 (March–June, 1923); William H. Glasson,
Federal Military Pensions in the United States (New York, 1918), 123–129; R.A.
Tenney, *Pension Laws* (Chicago, 1886), "Laws and Statutes Now in Force," Section
4692 Revised Statutes, July 14, 1862, and Section 4693, Revised Statutes, March 3,
1865, pp. 13–14; Wilson, *The Grand Army of the Republic Under Its First
Constitution,* 194–195, 202–203.
[75]Wis. G.A.R., *Proceedings,* 1867, pp. 18–20, 22–23.

300 veterans showed up. The flags drew attention because of their "honorable scars, received where bullets flew with remarkable celerity and alarming frequency," but the rally fizzled.[76]

Not only did the rally not attract many veterans, but local Democrats even made speeches proclaiming their hope that ex-Confederate soldiers might "again enjoy the rights of citizenship."[77] Iron Brigade veteran Alfred E. Haven, associate editor of the *La Crosse Evening Democrat*, lambasted the Bloody Shirt politicians and the battle flags which accompanied them. Haven explained that the Union cause had been "made unholy by political blood suckers" who dragged "from its grave the stinking carcass of a fratricidal struggle and use its bones to stir up strife. . . ."[78] He urged that the flags be returned to the "places from whence they came." "Peace in its fullest sense," concluded the Iron Brigade veteran, "cannot come while we delight in bringing in view scenes of the late war. . . . It needs no display of tattered flags. . . ."[79]

Washburn carried the state, although his administration was later hampered by the nationwide economic depression of 1873, unenviable association with the scandals of the Grant era, and passage of an unpopular liquor-control measure. The battle flags made an appearance at the Society of the Army of the Tennessee Convention held in Madison in July, 1872; but four years passed before they would again appear in public as a group.[80] During that time, Fairchild departed for a diplomatic post in Europe, while the GAR, like veterans' organizations across most parts of the nation, experienced a rapidly declining membership—dropping to a mere 253 in Wisconsin during 1875.[81] In 1873, the Democrats overwhelmingly captured the Wisconsin governorship and the Assembly. In 1874, they became the majority party in the U.S. House of Representatives. In 1876, Democrats also achieved majority

---

[76]*La Crosse Republican and Leader*, June 17, 1871; *Milwaukee Sentinel*, June 9, 10, 1871.

[77]*Ibid.*

[78]*La Crosse Evening Democrat*, June 10, 1871.

[79]*Ibid.*

[80]*Ibid.*; Society of the Army of the Tennessee, *Report of the Proceedings of the Society of the Army of the Tennessee at the Annual Meeting Held at Madison, Wisconsin July 3 and 4, 1872* (Cincinnati, 1877), 64–65; Durrie, *Madison*, 349–350; "Speech before Society of the Army of the Tennessee, July 4, 1872," in the Fairchild Papers.

[81]Wis. G.A.R., *Proceedings*, 1889, pp. 62–64, give figures for G.A.R. membership in Wisconsin from 1875 (the first year records were kept) to 1888.

in the U.S. Senate after winning the popular—but not the electoral—vote for the presidency.[82]

During the administration of Governor William R. Taylor of Dane County, the Democratically controlled Wisconsin legislature passed an act amending the 1870 battle flag preservation law. The act of March, 1875, required that Wisconsin's Civil War flags "shall not be removed" from their cases, "except as such removal may be required for their safety and better preservation."[83] The new law thus removed the Civil War flags from the political arena, as Democrats locked the artifacts of the Bloody Shirt into glass cases.

Democrats naturally recognized the potential of an ex-soldier voting bloc and they strove to offset the initial Republican advantage in appealing to the veteran element. When the "incarceration law" took the battle flags from the hands of Republican GAR men and Bloody Shirt politicians, the resurgent Democrats made an effort to court the veterans in order to enlarge their own party's following. Democratic veteran leaders espoused an end to war-generated bitterness between North and South. They emphasized the social aspect of military fraternal gatherings by sentimentally recollecting the comradeship shared by all Union soldiers regardless of their political affiliation.

There existed no shortage of popular Democratic veteran leaders in Wisconsin, moreover. Democratic veteran organizers included such men as ex-Brigadier General Harrison C. Hobart of Chilton, who had been speaker of the Assembly prior to the war. Hobart ran unsuccessfully for governor in 1860 and lost to Lucius Fairchild in 1865. Hobart became successful in Milwaukee political affairs during the 1870s, and he joined the Soldiers' and Sailors' National Union League as well as the GAR.[84]

---

[82]Ross, *Empty Sleeve*, 157–158; Lankevitch, "G.A.R. in New York State," 138; State of Wisconsin, *Legislative Manual for the State of Wisconsin* (Madison, 1873–1876), esp. 1873, 1874, 1875, and 1876, "Composition of Senate and Assembly." See also *Wisconsin Blue Book, 1981*, p. 703.

[83]*Annual Messages of Wisconsin Governors, 1874*, p. 9; *Laws of Wisconsin, 1875,* Chap. 142.

[84]*Soldiers' and Citizens' Album,* 2:743–745; *Wisconsin Necrology,* vol. 7, pp. 76–78; *Roster of Wisconsin Volunteers,* vol. 1, p. 192, and vol. 2, p. 164; Soldiers and Sailors National Union League Accounts of Members, General Records, 1866–1880.

George W. Peck had served with the Fourth Wisconsin Cavalry before he became a La Crosse newspaper editor and local politician. Peck was appointed chief clerk of the State Assembly in 1874. He later settled in Milwaukee after establishing a humorous newspaper, *Peck's Sun*. His style made him an entertaining speaker, much sought after among his fellow GAR members.[85]

Gabriel Bouck was a lawyer, banker, and merchant from Oshkosh who had been a prominent Democrat politician before 1861 when he organized a company of the Iron Brigade's Second Infantry. Promoted to command of the Eighteenth Regiment in 1862, Bouck used his abilities to convince many of his men to vote against the re-election of President Abraham Lincoln during 1864. Bouck became speaker of the Assembly in 1875 and served on the GAR's national council of administration. According to his Republican rivals, "as a stump speaker Col. Bouck has no superior. . . ."[86]

Ex-Brigadier General John B. Callis of Lancaster organized Company F of the Iron Brigade's Seventh Wisconsin Infantry regiment. Wounded at Second Bull Run and again very seriously at Gettysburg, the physically handicapped, North Carolina-born Callis was elected to the legislature during the 1874 Democratic sweep. He, too, was a GAR member.[87]

Gilbert M. Woodward of La Crosse had served with the Iron Brigade's Second Wisconsin before being wounded at Gettysburg. He was a prominent lawyer, local district attorney, and mayor. He had helped organize the La Crosse GAR post and was the principal ally of the state's foremost Democratic veteran politician, ex-Brigadier General Edward S. Bragg of Fond du Lac.[88]

After being wounded at Antietam, Bragg had risen to command of the Iron Brigade. President Andrew Johnson appointed him

---

[85] *Roster of Wisconsin Volunteers in the War of the Rebellion,* 769; *Soldiers and Citizens Album,* 2:771–772; *Wisconsin Necrology,* vol. 15, pp. 164–165.

[86] *Wisconsin State Journal,* February 22, 1904; *Roster of Wisconsin Volunteers in the War of the Rebellion,* vol. 1, p. 359, vol. 2, p. 83. Also see the Jerome A. Watrous Papers, 1864–1922, Clippings, Archives, Wisconsin Veterans Museum; J.M. Rusk to Angus Cameron, May 25, 1882, in the Jeremiah M. Rusk Papers, Wisconsin State Archives; *Oshkosh Northwestern,* August 28, 1866; and Beath, *Grand Army of the Republic,* 152.

[87] *Soldiers and Citizens Album,* 2:391; *Roster of Wisconsin Volunteers in the War of the Rebellion,* vol. 1, p. 350.

[88] *Wisconsin Necrology,* vol. 14, pp. 16–24; *Roster of Wisconsin Volunteers in the War of the Rebellion,* vol. 1, p. 350.

postmaster at Fond du Lac in 1866. Bragg served as state senator between 1868 and 1872 before voters sent him to Congress for three consecutive terms beginning in 1876.[89]

Democratic control of the Wisconsin Assembly and statehouse lasted two years until Harrison Ludington, the Republican mayor of Milwaukee, helped defeat Governor Taylor and the Democrats by the narrowest of margins.[90] Shortly after Ludington took office in 1876, legislators amended the act which prohibited state Civil War flags from leaving their cases. The 1876 legislation authorized two uses for the battle flags: they could now attend festivities associated with the nation's Centennial, and more importantly, "upon application of the officers commanding," they could be "used at reunions of. . . regiments, batteries, or detachments. . .or [by] any military or regimental organization."[91]

The 1876 law freed the battle flags from their cases and democratized their use. For the next decade, the flags traveled about the state to reunions and celebrations. Leaders of the moribund GAR focused on the social programs, fraternal parades, and "camp fires" that became popular gatherings. The battle flags helped attract veterans and other citizens to these events (and, incidentally, helped the GAR survive long enough to achieve a reorganization and a luxurious regeneration during the 1880s). Battle flags appeared at Centennial celebrations in Madison, La Crosse, Sheboygan, Oconomowoc, Sturgeon Bay, Menasha, Oconto, and Kewaskum. In addition to the historic banners, Centennial celebrators borrowed surplus Civil War tents, muskets, and the surplus cannons parked around the capitol.[92] Centennial festivities were ostensibly nonpartisan events, but

---

[89] *Roster of the Wisconsin Volunteers in the War of the Rebellion,* vol. 1, p. 494, 513; Jerome A. Watrous Papers, Civil War Materials, Wisconsin State Archives; George R. Farnum, "Edward S. Bragg Soldier, Lawyer, Statesman," in the *American Bar Association Journal,* 30: 21–22 (January, 1944); Bragg to Dear Wife, December 2, 1882, in the Edward S. Bragg Papers, Wisconsin State Archives; *Milwaukee Sentinel,* September 18, 1882. Also see Edward L. Gambill, "A Biography of Edward S. Bragg" (masters thesis, University of Wisconsin, 1960), *passim.*

[90] *Wisconsin Blue Book, 1981,* p. 703. Less than 1,000 votes separated Taylor and Ludington in 1875.

[91] *Laws of Wisconsin, 1876,* Chap. 208.

[92] *Wisconsin State Journal,* July 5, 1876. See also P.C. Priest to Harrison Ludington, May 1, 1876; Nathan Cole to Ludington, May 19, 1876; Floyd C. Babcock to Ludington, June 21, 1876; R.M. Wright to Ludington, June 7, 1876; E.B. Crofoot to Ludington, June 22, 1876; and N. Thatcher to Ludington, June 5, 1876; all in Gov. Military Corr.

WHi (x3) 39448

Unidentified GAR reunion, in the 1880s.

local politicians such as George Beyer, an insurance agent from Oconto and an ex-officer in the Thirty-ninth Wisconsin Infantry, viewed the gatherings differently. Beyer noted in a letter to Republican party boss Elisha W. Keyes of Madison that he hoped the cannons and muskets sent by the governor would be helpful "next fall" because "whoever will be in hearing of it will hear it belch forth a good sound Republican victory."[93]

Flags—including several from the Iron Brigade— attended veterans' reunions at Menomonie in 1877 and at Durand in 1878. In 1879 they were present at the reunion of the Association of Soldiers and Veterans of Dunn, Pepin, Pierce, and Buffalo counties held in Menomonie. In May 1879, the flags of the Second, Eighth, and Thirty-first Infantry were taken to a Memorial Day gathering in Prairie Du Chien.[94] The fact that at least one of the Iron Brigade flags was "not in condition to be used" did not phase reunion organizers. As Militus Knight, a veteran of the Thirtieth Wisconsin and clerk of Pepin County, explained to Governor William E. Smith, "there are a good many men here that were in that Brigade [Iron Brigade], and they are *more than*

---

[93]George Beyer to E.W. Keyes, June 7, 1876, in Gov. Military Corr.

[94]George Tonnar to Ludington, May 4, 1877; Militus Knight to Gov. William E. Smith, May 3, 1878; N. Brush and E.L. Doolittle to William E. Smith, August 29, 1879; George Tonnar to W.E. Smith, September 16, 1879; William H. Evans to William E. Smith, May 28, 1879; George H. Otis to William E. Smith, May 21, 1879, all in Gov. Military Corr.

anxious to see the flag." Knight advised the governor to cover the tattered flag with cotton and promised that it would not be unfurled at the reunion in recognition of its deteriorated condition.[95]

Indeed, the tempo of Civil War veterans and other military gatherings in Wisconsin, as elsewhere, increased dramatically as the decade of the 1870s drew to a close. In Hartford, Connecticut, for example, when state battle flags were transferred to newly constructed cases in the capitol from their depository at the local armory in September, 1879, approximately 100,000 citizens showed up to watch and cheer as the flags moved by. A *New York Times* story called it "the greatest popular demonstration ever witnessed in the State."[96] A reunion sponsored by the Chicago Union Veterans Club likewise drew crowds of over 100,000 when it gathered in Aurora, Illinois, in the late summer of 1879.[97]

Not only did reunions gain in popularity and attendance, but in Wisconsin, as in other states, numerous militia units also sprang up. "At no time since the war," reported Adjutant General Edwin E. Bryant in September, 1879, "has so much interest been manifested in military organizations as at present. Military drills and parades are becoming an important feature at fairs and other public gatherings."[98] Surplus war material found new uses as the militia companies formed, while governors found additional patronage outlets in the appointment of local officers.[99]

The stage was now set for the transformation of veterans' groups from scattered soldier clubs and the nearly defunct GAR—whose membership in Wisconsin during 1879 had dwindled to 135— into a national lobby able to influence elections and, therefore, legislation and the composition of governmental agencies.[100] The closely matched strength of the major political parties, and especially the popular social aspect of the military gatherings,

---

[95]Militus Knight to G.W. Burchard, September 15, 1879, Gov. Military Corr.

[96]*New York Times,* September 20, 1879; *History of Battle Flag Day, September 17, 1879* (Hartford, Connecticut, 1879), 28–29.

[97]Chicago Union Veterans Club to Gov. William Smith, August 16, 1879, Department of Executive, Administration, Civil War Memorials, Wisconsin State Archives; *Chicago Tribune,* August 22, 23, 1879.

[98]*Rpt. Wis. Adj. Gen., 1879,* p.3.

[99]Wis. QMG, General Correspondence, 1863–1882, Wisconsin State Archives, *passim*; Jerry M. Cooper, "The Wisconsin Militia, 1832–1900" (master's thesis, University of Wisconsin, 1968), 124, 130.

[100]Wis. G.A.R., *Proceedings,* 1889, pp. 62–64.

combined to bring forth a new era in veterans' affairs. The battle flags played a role in these developments, because, as one Wisconsin reunion organizer put it, the veterans "have a desire to march under the old flags once more."[101]

Other factors contributed to the revived interest in soldiers' organizations. One of these was increased leisure time, as the boys of 1861–1865 approached their middle years and had established themselves economically. The national penchant for joining groups revealed itself in 260 new secret organizations, including numerous veterans' societies, which formed during

Photo courtesy Craig L. Buswell

The William A. Barstow GAR Post 88, Kendall, Wisconsin, about 1885.

1880–1896. Older fraternal orders such as the Odd Fellows also experienced rapid growth. Nostalgic memories of the war experience, which included heady recollections of comradeship, heroism, and sacrifice—as one veteran put it in 1880, "the most precious memories of our lives"—no doubt encouraged soldiers' organization membership, along with the growing popularity of Memorial Day as a holiday. Perhaps most important, however, was a revival of interest in national Civil War pensions for Union veterans, together with an appreciation of the need for a strong lobbying organization to obtain them. The Arrears Act of January 25, 1879, for example, established the precedent for sub-

---

[101]William H. Evans to William E. Smith, May 28, 1879, Gov. Military Corr.

stantially broadening existing pension legislation, making available sizable chunks of "arrears" (ranging from $953.62 to $1,121.51) for 138,195 ex-soldiers not previously qualified to receive payments.[102] In other words, a series of favorable circumstances operated to encourage and rejuvenate veterans' organizations at this particular juncture. And, as in every age, whenever and wherever crowds of voters gathered or organized, politicians were sure to be found.

Wisconsin veterans convincingly demonstrated their collective strength in June, 1880. Following a year of intense planning, veteran activists formed the Wisconsin Soldiers' and Sailors' Reunion Association. The GAR—after repudiating overt political involvement, graded membership, and its Radial Republican views—undertook a compilation of names and addresses of veterans residing in Wisconsin. C.K. Pier, a GAR member from Fond du Lac undertook the census with the help of Griff J. Thomas, the state commander, who was also Fairchild's campaign manager and the postmaster at Berlin. The Milwaukee Chamber of Commerce and the Merchants' Association of Milwaukee influenced the choice of location for the social reunion by securing space for a tent camp north of the city's waterworks along the lake front.[103]

A bipartisan host of soldier-politicians helped veterans organize. Democrats Harrison Hobart, George Peck, Gabe Bouck, Edward Bragg, and William F. Vilas became active in the giant

---

[102]B.H. Meyer, "Fraternal Beneficiary Societies in the United States," in the *American Journal of Sociology,* 6:655 (March, 1901); Rood, "Wisconsin G.A.R.," 293; Dearing, *Veterans in Politics,* 191–193, 243–246; Heck, *Minnesota Veterans,* 11, 23; Lankevitch, "G.A.R. in New York State," 15–17, 104; Glasson, *Federal Military Pensions,* 148–149, 166; William H. Glasson, *History of Military Pension Legislation in the United States* (New York, 1900), 88–109; Tenney, *Pension Laws,* 60–63; Speech of Col. E. F. Brown of Ohio, *Journal of the National G.A.R. Encampment, 1880* (Columbus, 1881), 661–662; Edward R. Noyes, "The Ohio G.A.R. and Politics from 1866–1900," in the *Ohio State Archeological and Historical Quarterly,* 55:79 (April–June, 1946), 79; *Milwaukee Sentinel,* June 7, 1880; Stuart McConnell, *Glorious Contentment: The Grand Army of the Republic 1865–1900* (Chappel Hill, 1992), 237.

[103]Rood, "Wisconsin G.A.R.," 292–293; C.K. Pier, *Wisconsin Soldiers' and Sailors' Reunion Roster* (Fond du Lac, 1880), 234; Flower, *Milwaukee,* 2:784; Dearing, *Veterans in Politics,* 185; Lankevitch, "G.A.R. in New York State," 75; "Men Who Have Been at the Head of the Grand Army in Wisconsin," no date, in the Watrous Papers, Wisconsin State Archives; Beath, *Grand Army of the Republic,* 540; *Milwaukee Sentinel,* June 7, 1880; Wallace Davies, "Was Lucius Fairchild a Demogogue?" in the *Wisconsin Magazine of History,* 31:419 (June, 1948).

Photo by E.D. Bangs. WHi (x3) 9306

Veterans of the 1st Wisconsin Cavalry in Milwaukee, about 1880.

reunion effort, as did Republicans such as ex-Congressman Jerry Rusk, chairman of the House Committee on Invalid Pensions in 1876 and soon to be gubernatorial candidate; ex-Congressman Halbert Paine; ex-governor (and now University Regent) Cadwallader C. Washburn; Charles King, son of Rufus King, who had been the original commander of the Iron Brigade; and John Starkweather, ex-colonel of the First Wisconsin Infantry.[104]

Governor William E. Smith supported the veterans by speaking on behalf of the reunion. The governor also authorized State Quartermaster General Edwin Bryant to "thoroughly repair" the state battle flags which would be prominently displayed during the gathering.[105] In fact, the veterans were urged to attend the five-day affair because the flags would be in attendance: "Let the storm tattered flags riven by shot and shell on a hundred fields of battle, once more be unfolded to the breeze. . . ."[106]

The Great Reunion took place June 7–12, 1880. Although the weather was disagreeably warm, muggy, and frequently rainy, the gathering attracted huge crowds. Veterans, families, spectators, and hucksters doubled Milwaukee's population of 150,000. Citizens who "came to see the old veterans" packed every hotel

---

[104]Pier, *Reunion Roster,* 270–273; Delegation of Veterans of the Mexican War to J.M. Rusk, January 13, 1875, in the Rusk Papers, Correspondence, box 1; Rusk to Friend Charles P. Seymour, February 9, 1877, *ibid.*

[105]Wisconsin Soldiers Reunion Executive Committee to Gov. Smith, April 19, 1880, Gov. Military Corr.; *Rpt. Wis. QMG, 1880,* p. 3; Pier, *Reunion Roster,* 273.

[106]Pier, *Reunion Roster,* 273; *Racine Journal,* June 2, 1880; *Milwaukee Sentinel,* June 7, 1880.

in the city as well as those in nearby Racine, Waukesha, and Oconomowoc. Food supplies ran short. As one reporter noted, "it was a difficult matter to get square meals or anything better than rye bread and beer."[107] The tent camp for veterans at North Point sheltered between 20,000 and 30,000 veterans in rain-soaked, muddy conditions that probably recalled old campaigns. Each ex-soldier provided his own blanket, tin cup, plate, and eating utensils, as well as fifty cents per day. The veterans brought whatever parts of their old uniforms they still possessed—or could fit into—and were required to supply army-type slouch hats or fatigue caps. Milwaukee residents decorated their homes with flowers and banners.[108]

On June 9, a giant parade of "the greatest reunion of soldiers held anywhere since the war" took place.[109] Former President Grant and General Philip H. Sheridan were the guests of honor. They led the procession of members of Wisconsin regiments, numbering about 25,000 men, while more than 100,000 viewers cheered. It was "a great seething surging mass of humanity," recorded the *Milwaukee Sentinel*: "The men who had forgotten for fifteen years that they were heroes . . . have now been reminded of it again."[110] As usual, the battle flags seemed to capture the emotional essence of the Civil War experience. The *Sentinel's* reporter observed: "Hats went off as the column swung by, and cheers went up that seemed to make the ground tremble. When the flags torn by shot and shell were borne by, a quiver went through the vast assemblage and a moment after, the wildest excitement prevailed."[111]

On June 12, the veterans broke camp and the battle flags were returned to their glass cases in the "state historical rooms" at the capitol.[112] The flags had thus served again to inspire veterans and other citizens. They had been repaired for the second time since returning from the war. Nor did they rest long in their cases. In September, selected banners were displayed at a reunion in Port Washington. In October, flags and cannon went to Chilton "for use of the Garfield and Arthur Club and the town generally." In June, 1881, "cannon, tents, and colors" traveled to

---

[107]*Milwaukee Sentinel*, June 12, 1880.
[108]*Ibid.*; *Racine Journal*, June 2, 1880; Flower, *Milwaukee*, 2:784.
[109]Watrous Papers, Wisconsin Veterans Museum, Clippings.
[110]*Milwaukee Sentinel*, June 12, 1880; Dearing, *Veterans in Politics*, 263.
[111]*Milwaukee Sentinel*, June 11, 1880.
[112]*Rpt. Wis. QMG, 1880*, p. 3.

Sturgeon Bay for a local reunion.[113]

The most important effects of the Great Reunion of 1880, other than demonstrating the numerical strength and popular support that organized veterans could generate, was in the creation of regimental associations. The formal organization of these associations was planned in advance by reunion leaders.[114] The regimental associations formed a local grapevine through which the ex-soldiers might be rallied or informed on issues that, like pensions, would be of particular interest to them. They could be marshalled for social gatherings, or for future organizing into the ranks of the Grand Army of the Republic. With good reason, one reunion organizer noted that the "boys have grown more thoughtful. Hence it is that . . . reunions are becoming more general, and we look forward to them with deeper interest as the years wear away."[115]

The case of the Iron Brigade illustrates the phenomenon. During the Great Reunion, Iron Brigade veterans formed the Iron Brigade Association, a "semi-civic society." Organizers included Iron Brigade members and such Fairchild allies as James Kellogg, Joseph H. Marston of Appleton, and Jerome A. Watrous, a newspaperman and professional writer from Fond du Lac who moved to Milwaukee in 1879 where he became associate editor and later editor-in-chief of the *Milwaukee Telegraph*. Over the next several decades, Watrous acted as the secretary of the Iron Brigade Association as well as the "pen" of the state GAR, eventually becoming its commander. Representatives from the Iron Brigade's Nineteenth Indiana and Twenty-fourth Michigan regiments were also present.[116]

The ex-soldiers chose as president of their association General John Gibbon, a Regular Army officer who had commanded the Iron Brigade at Gainesville, South Mountain, and Antietam. Because Gibbon was stationed on the Pacific Coast and could therefore not be expected to attend reunions on a regular basis, the

---

[113]E.R. Blake to Governor Smith, September 9, 1880; D.G. Marsh to Secretary of State, October 15, 1880; both in Gov. Military Corr.
[114]*Racine Journal*, June 2, 1880; *Milwaukee Sentinel*, June 11, 1880.
[115]Pier, *Reunion Roster*, 247.
[116]*Milwaukee Sentinel*, June 9, 11, 12, 1880; *National Tribune*, June 15, 1922; J.A. Watrous, *Richard Epps and Other Stories* (Milwaukee, 1906); J.A. Watrous, ed., *Memories of Milwaukee County* (2 vols., Milwaukee, 1909).

Photo by E.R. Curtis. Wisconsin Veterans Museum

***Iron Brigade Association leaders, about 1885. From the left: Lucius
Fairchild, Edward Bragg, and John Gibbon.***

choice of first vice-president became crucial. (It was he who
selected the date and site of the group's reunions.) Congressman Edward S. Bragg was elected to fill the important post, and
each of the five regiments in the brigade provided a vice-president with less power than the senior vice-president.[117]

Bragg chose to hold the first reunion of the Iron Brigade Association in Milwaukee during September, 1882. The brigade's battle
flags were "nailed to the wall" of the Stanley and Camp Jewelry
Store on Wisconsin Avenue and Broadway, headquarters of the

---

[117]*Milwaukee Sentinel,* July 23, 1882.

reunion association, to "give a martial appearance." As one veteran said to a *Sentinel* reporter: "Twenty years ago I saw that old flag on South Mountain and it was a sorry day for some of our boys."[118] The general meeting took place at City Hall, and some 250 of the Iron Brigade's approximately 700 survivors attended. Governor Rusk, Congressman Bragg, and General Gibbon addressed the assembled veterans. So did Lucius Fairchild, who had returned home after spending a decade in diplomatic posts in Europe. Fairchild became the association's second vice-president. The speakers urged Iron Brigade members to support future reunions and to join the GAR.[119]

WHi (x3) 41504

The veterans received commemorative Iron Brigade cigars, while Hattie M. Aubrey, the teen-aged daughter of Cullen "Doc" Aubrey, a newspaper boy attached to the Iron Brigade during the war, recited a poem and presented a handmade white silk guidon to the men. Father and daughter were elected honorary members of the Iron Brigade Association.[120]

Hattie M. Aubery, Daughter of the Iron Brigade, in 1882 with the Tiffany flag.

Bragg chose La Crosse for the next reunion. The Fond du Lac Democrat stressed the social, nonpolitical aspect of the event, promising good fellowship and "entertainment for all."[121] He advertised the presence of the Civil War flags to encourage attendance. "The flags of the . . . old brigade will be present," General Bragg noted. "It will

[118] *Ibid.*, September 15, 1882.

[119] *Ibid.*, September 18, 21, 1882; John Stahel to J.M. Rusk, June 1, 1882; both in Gov. Military Corr.

[120] *Milwaukee Sentinel*, September 21, 1882; Cullen B. "Doc" Aubery, *Echoes From the Marches of the Famous Iron Brigade* (Milwaukee, n.d.) 61, 67. See also Cullen B. Aubery, *Twenty-Five Years on the Streets of Milwaukee After Dark; Together with Sketches and Experiences as a Newsboy in the Army of the Potomac* (Milwaukee, 1897); and Cullen B. Aubery, *Recollections of a Newsboy in the Army of the Potomac, 1861–1865* (n.p., n.d.); Ross, *Empty Sleeve*, 186.

[121] *Milwaukee Sentinel*, August 7, 15, 1883.

do us all good to see those torn and tattered battle flags." The governor of Michigan, however, refused to allow the flags of the Twenty-fourth Michigan to appear at La Crosse because "the flags are so old and rotten that but a few handling would entirely destroy them."[122]

The reunion was well-attended despite the absence of the Michigan flags. Bragg, Rogers, and Watrous made opening addresses to the veterans assembled in Germania Hall. General John Callis of Lancaster sent a regretful letter explaining that the crippling effects of multiple wounds prevented his own appearance. But the Lancaster politician's comments were read to the veterans. Callis summarized the Democratic position on the Civil War experience, on veterans' gatherings, and on what was hoped for in the future. He explained that the Union soldiers of 1861– 1865, "regardless of . . . political opinions or party affinities," had been "actuated by . . . patriotism and love of country: In short we had no political axes to grind. . . ." The war, its suffering, and the bonds of comradeship it created could never be forgotten, but "now that the war is over. . . I for one can freely forgive" the "misguided" Confederates. Callis concluded with an appeal to end postwar bitterness: "*No More Bloody Shirt. . . of that I have had quite too much.*"[123]

Reunion activities included other pleasantries. The veterans spent the morning of September 14 listening to poems, recitals by local glee clubs, and singing "The Battle Cry of Freedom—which made the walls tremble." As evidence of the new democratic spirit among the veterans, Bragg invited Mickey Sullivan, a private during the war, to present his humorous stories of life in the ranks of the Iron Brigade. Sullivan became the first enlisted man to formally participate in the reunion association's programs. His appearance set a notable precedent. Subsequent Iron Brigade reunions always featured non-officer presentations.[124]

A parade of Iron Brigade veterans attracted "great throngs of

---

[122]*Ibid.*, August 15, 1883; E.S. Bragg and J.A. Watrous, "Reunion of the Iron Brigade," LaCrosse, August 7, 1883 (n.p., n.d.); W. Shakespeare to J.A. Watrous, August 30, 1883, in Secretary of State, Administrative Department, Elections and Records, Iron Brigade Reunion, 1883–1884, Wisconsin State Archives. Cited hereinafter as Sec. of State, Elections and Records.

[123]John B. Callis to Comrades of the Iron Brigade, September 10, 1883, Sec. of State, Elections and Records; Callis to J.A. Watrous, September 18, 1883, *ibid.*

[124]*La Crosse Morning Chronicle,* September 15, 1883; *LaCrosse Republican and Leader,* September 15, 1883.

citizens" along its route. The Wisconsin regimental battle flags accompanied the veterans in line while bands and local militia companies marched in support. The *Milwaukee Sentinel* called it an "imposing spectacle."[125] Dancing and singing provided the evening's entertainment. Under Chinese lanterns and electric lights, Bragg did solo performances of "Tenting On the Old Camp Ground" and the "Red, White, and Blue." "Good feelings ruled supreme at this reunion," concluded the editor of the *La Crosse Republican and Leader*.[126]

Cracks in the facade of social fellowship of the Iron Brigade Association, and in the nonpolitical orientation of military fraternal organizations, began to appear in 1884. In January, Lucius Fairchild, who was considering a run for the U.S. Senate, and several other Iron Brigade members, invited the association to hold its reunion in Madison. However, after a lengthy delay, Bragg declined their offer and instead chose Lancaster as the site of the meeting.[127] Politics may well have influenced the Democratic senior vice-president's decision, since the 1884 presidential election promised to be yet another exceptionally close contest between the major political parties. Grover Cleveland, Democrat of New York, was an attractive candidate, and shortly thereafter he became president by a bare majority.

In any case, Lancaster prepared to host the Iron Brigade reunion on August 28, the anniversary of the battle of Gainesville. Nearly 200 veterans attended the gathering. When Lucius Fairchild arrived in accompaniment with Watrous, Allen, and Rufus Dawes, cheering local citizens carried the ex-governor to a waiting carriage and took him to Hyde's Opera House for the meeting.[128] Rain prevented a parade, but the veterans attentively listened to speeches. As usual, the battle flags were attached to the windows of the hall.[129]

John Callis touched off the speechmaking. The ailing Lancaster Democrat greeted the veterans and sentimentally reminded them that the reunion meeting had "no political significance other than to teach the world. . . that loyalty to this government and

---

[125]*Milwaukee Sentinel,* September 14, 1883.
[126]*La Crosse Republican and Leader,* September 15, 1883.
[127]*Milwaukee Sentinel,* January 14, 1884; *Grant County Herald,* August 1, September 4, 1884.
[128]*Ibid.,* September 4, 1884; Iron Brigade Reunion, 1883–1884, Sec. of State, Elections and Records.
[129]*Milwaukee Sentinel,* August 29, 1884.

the union. . . has been the shibboleth of our faith in, and love for one another."[130] Gil Woodward then presented a humorous talk that poked fun at Fairchild's performance at Second Bull Run. Phil Cheek, Jr., a Baraboo attorney and an ex-private in the Sixth Wisconsin, made a humorous speech as the non-officer's presentation. He also harangued the assembled veterans, urging them to join the GAR.[131]

Cheek, who "takes the cake for lively speech making," was state commander of the GAR, and he presided over the organization's phenomenal resurgence in Wisconsin.[132] A "whirlwind cyclonic campaigner," Cheek became known as the GAR's "hustler in chief." During his first term as state commander, for example, membership rose 185 per cent to 5,979. By the end of 1884, when he stepped down, membership totaled 9,165. During Cheek's administration, GAR membership in Wisconsin rose at three times the national rate.[133]

After the official meeting at Lancaster, Iron Brigade veterans attended a "camp fire"—an evening picnic replete with songs and stories. Afterward, Lucius Fairchild invited the association to hold its next reunion in Madison.[134]

During early 1885, Fairchild made the rounds of local veterans' reunions, such as those hosted by Company D of the Seventh Wisconsin in Stoughton and another in Berlin shortly thereafter, urging members to attend the gathering in Madison during September.[135] Fairchild's presence at these local affairs was always appreciated. As he explained to a family member: "I am now a 'buster' on campfire speeches—as I have been since my return from Europe. . . ,and the boys go off their heads in cheering."[136]

Fairchild carefully organized the Madison reunion of the Iron

[130] *Grant County Herald,* September 4, 1884.

[131] *Ibid.*; Philip Cheek and Mair Pointon, *History of the Sauk County Riflemen, Known as Company "A," Sixth Wisconsin Veterans Volunteer Infantry* (Baraboo, 1909), 10.

[132] "Men Who Have Been at the Head of the Grand Army in Wisconsin," in the Watrous Papers, Wisconsin State Archives.

[133] Wis. G.A.R., *Proceedings,* 1889, pp. 62–65; *Journal of National G.A.R. Encampment,* 1883, pp. 5–6. National GAR membership was 60,654 in 1880; 131,900 in 1882; and 273,174 in 1884. See *Milwaukee Sentinel,* August 27, 1889.

[134] *Grant County Herald,* September 4, 1884.

[135] D.F. Tipple to Lucius Fairchild, January 2, 1885; Griff J. Thomas to Fairchild, February 9, 1885; both in the Fairchild Papers.

[136] Fairchild to Dear Charlie, April 4, 1886, *ibid.*

Photo by J. M. Fowler. Wisconsin Veterans Museum

The Iron Brigade Association Reunion in the state capitol in 1885.

Brigade Association. The governors of Michigan and Indiana agreed to be there, as did Congressman Robert M. La Follette. Railroad discounts helped encourage attendance. Some 350 Iron Brigade veterans showed up for the elaborate two-day reunion. The Assembly Chamber in the state capitol provided seating for the official meeting, while Camp Randall was the site of a "Bean Banquet."[137] Iron Brigade member and State Adjutant General Chandler P. Chapman of Madison designed a special badge consisting of a "five armed iron Maltese Cross suspended by a blue ribbon" to give each Iron Brigade veteran attending the reunion.[138]

About 1,000 veterans and spectators crammed the packed Assembly Chamber as General Bragg introduced Jerry Rusk, "the soldier-governor," who gave a welcoming speech. Rusk—who was to be Wisconsin's second three-term governor—declared that he "loved all Union soldiers." The "bebadged crowd" next called on General Fairchild to give an extemporaneous speech, responding with "three cheers" at its conclusion. Fairchild noted that other duties interfered with his position as second vice-president of the Iron Brigade Association and requested that Gil Woodward replace him. Various GAR representatives urged veterans to join their ranks.[139] Tom Kerr, an "ardent Democrat" from Milwaukee who rose from private to lieutenant colonel in the

---

[137]*Milwaukee Sentinel*, August 2, September 12, 1885; *Wisconsin State Journal*, September 15, 16, 1885.

[138]*Milwaukee Sentinel,* September 16, 17, 1885.

[139]*Wisconsin State Journal,* September 16, 1885; *Milwaukee Sentinel*, September 16, 1885.

Sixth Wisconsin, while being wounded on several occasions, gave the enlisted man's presentation.[140] Two Iron Brigade flags stood behind the speakers, while "around the chamber extending out over the auditorium, are thirteen regimental flags, whose tattered appearance and half obliterated inscriptions tell of many a hard fought battle. . . ."[141]

Fairchild's decision to remove himself from the second vice-presidency was not commented upon in the press. But it meant that the ex-governor was now at liberty to seek higher office within the Iron Brigade Association, in opposition to the Democrat, Edward Bragg. The Republican State Senator Levi E. Pond of Westfield, a GAR activist and Iron Brigade veteran, confidentially noted to Fairchild the following July: "Do you think that General Bragg ought to be continued in his present office in the Iron Brigade Association? I do not, for I am disgruntled with some of his speeches and acts in Congress. He seems to have a greater loyalty to party than to the old soldiery."[142]

Fairchild did seek high office in the GAR. He became state commander in 1886 and national commander in 1887, by which time GAR membership totalled nearly 400,000.[143] Fairchild strongly supported pension legislation and along with other GAR members, such as William T. Sherman, revived the Bloody Shirt issue in opposition to Democratic President Cleveland. Fairchild, the GAR, and Bloody Shirt activists helped influence the course of national veterans' politics during the latter 1880s, particularly during the presidential election of 1888.[144]

In some respects, Democratic politicians provided their Repub-

[140]*Madison Democrat,* September 16, 1885.
[141]*Wisconsin State Journal,* September 15, 16, 1885.
[142]L.E. Pond to Fairchild, July 15, 1886, in the Fairchild Papers; *Soldiers and Citizens Album,* 2:398.
[143]Lucius Fairchild to the Department of Wisconsin G.A.R. members, March 30, 1886, in the Fairchild Papers; Beath, *Grand Army of the Republic,* 325, 332, 540; J.M. Rusk to S.S. Burdette, March 15, 1886, in the Rusk Papers.
[144]Dearing, *Veterans in Politics,* 321–332, 325, 329, 339; Donald L. McMurry, "The Soldier Vote in Iowa in the Election of 1888," in the *Iowa Journal of History and Politics,* 18:343 (July, 1920); Donald L. McMurry, "The Political Significance of the Pension Question, 1885–1897," in the *Mississippi Valley Historical Review,* 9:19 (1921–1922); Edward Noyes, "The Ohio G.A.R. and Politics," *Ohio Historical Quarterly,* 79; John A. Logan, *The Great Conspiracy* (New York, 1886), 658–669; *Journal of the National G.A.R. Encampment,* 1887, pp. 40–45. For modern views of pension questions see Richard F. Bensel, *Sectionalism and American Political Development, 1880–1980* (Madison, 1984); McConnell, *Glorious Contentment,* 220; and Theda Skocpol, *Protecting Soldiers and Mothers: The Political Origins of Social Policy in the United States* (Cambridge, 1992), 1–3.

Wisconsin Veterans Museum

The Iron Brigade Association Reunion in Oshkosh in 1886.

lican critics with the excuse they sought to reintroduce politics, however subtly, into local and national veterans' affairs. At the 1886 Iron Brigade Reunion Association meeting held in Oshkosh during late August, for example, Democrats monopolized the proceedings. Bragg selected the meeting date to partly conflict with the state GAR encampment in Lake Geneva. The fiery ex-Iron Brigade commander, who was running for Congress in the Second District, opened the well-attended meetings by eulogizing General George B. McClellan, the Democratic candidate in 1864. Gabe Bouck made a speech before introducing Milwaukee Democrat George W. Peck, who presented a series of humorous (and racist) stories. Only partly in jest, Gil Woodward, the Democratic gubernatorial candidate, made a speech in which he called Phil Cheek, the state GAR adjutant, a liar.[145]

Iron Brigade survivors marched behind their Civil War banners on September 1. "The tattered war colors were cheered at different points along the march," reported the *Oshkosh Northwestern*.[146] Photographers Cook Ely and O.H. Mazer recorded

---

[145] *Oshkosh Northwestern,* August 31, September 1, 1886; *Milwaukee Sentinel,* August 29, 31, 1886.

the event. An evening ball demonstrated "that the old boys had not forgotten how to dance."[147] But Fairchild and Bragg did not greet each other, for both were preparing for the contest they must have known lay ahead.

President Cleveland opened the next round in a struggle which marked the re-entry of organized veterans into politics. In early 1887, Cleveland signed a pension bill for Mexican War veterans while vetoing the Dependent Pension Bill for Civil War soldiers.[148] Mexican War pension applicants, furthermore, did not have to prove that they had not borne arms against the United States during 1861–1865, thus paving the way for ex-Confederates to receive payments. GAR activists responded quickly. Democrats like Bragg, Callis, and Gibbon supported the president's actions. Republicans, on the other hand, used the veto to show that Cleveland and the Democrats were "Rebels at heart."[149] "Now who are those Mexican soldiers?" rhetorically asked a Massachusetts GAR man in 1887: "I think that you will agree. . . that 4/5 of the pensioners of the Mexican War were men that you and I fought against [in the Civil War]; and the first man who received a pension under the Act was a rebel Briga-dier General. And I tell you, when we see those men who fought against us taking money out of the treasury of the United States that we made it possible to put in there, it is time we made an earnest demand for what we believe to be our rights."[150]

Commander Fairchild requested that all of the nearly 400,000 GAR members and nearly 1,000,000 other Union veterans still alive write to their Congressmen and express their opinions concerning the veto of the Dependent Pension Bill. As a nomi-nally nonpartisan organization, the GAR took no official posi-tion on the matter—probably in recognition of its approximately

[146]*Oshkosh Northwestern,* September 1, 1886.
[147]*Ibid.,* August 31, September 2, 1886.
[148]Grover Cleveland to House of Representatives, February 3, 11, 1887, in James D. Richardson, ed., *Messages and Papers of the Presidents,* vol. 8 (Washington, 1898), 543, 549–557.
[149]*Evening Wisconsin* (Madison), February 17, 1887; *Milwaukee Sentinel,* September 15, 1887; John Gibbon to E.S. Bragg, July 28, 1887, in the Bragg Papers; L.E. Peterson to Lucius Fairchild, June 18, 1887, in the Fairchild Papers.
[150]*Journal of the National G.A.R. Encampment,* 1887, pp. 219–220.

25 percent Democratic membership.[151]

Presidential vetoes of other Civil War pension bills further contributed to Cleveland's reputation as being unfriendly to Union veterans, as did his decision not to attend the 1887 national encampment of the Grand Army of the Republic, his much-publicized fishing trip on Memorial Day, and his appointment of ex-Confederate officers to governmental positions, including the Supreme Court.[152] Many veterans no doubt recalled that Cleveland had hired a substitute to serve in his stead during the war.

But the final act which unified many veterans against Grover Cleveland involved Civil War battle flags—Confederate ones. In June, the president directed the secretary of war to return all captured Confederate banners in federal possession to the respective Southern states. When the order became public, GAR National Commander Lucius Fairchild was on a speaking tour of posts in the East.[153] Appearing before the Alexander Hamilton Post of Harlem, New York, on June 15, on the occasion of the completion of a Memorial Hall to house that state's Civil War flags, the one-armed Fairchild delivered an angry and unforgettable speech denouncing President Cleveland's action: "May God palsy the hand that wrote the order! May God palsy the brain that conceived it! And may God palsy the tongue that dictated it! I appeal to the sentiment of the nation to prevent this sacrilege."[154]

"I have never seen a body of men more excited than were the old soldiers there," Fairchild told his wife. "Many. . . stood with their eyes full of tears. . . ."[155] Fairchild's "three palsies" speech received tremendous national attention, drawing both criticism and praise. The Wisconsin GAR supported Fairchild, as did other state GAR organizations, although the national GAR commandery

---

[151]National Headquarters G.A.R., Circular No. 4, 1887, in the Fairchild Papers; *Milwaukee Sentinel*, February 17, 1887; Wis. G.A.R., *Proceedings*, 1888, pp. 24–25; Robert M. La Follette to Lucius Fairchild, February 20, 1887, in the Fairchild Papers; Lucius Fairchild to *Madison Democrat*, February 16, 1887, *ibid.*, Scrapbooks, reel 2; John C. Black to S.S. Burdett, August 5, 1885, *Journal of the National G.A.R. Encampment*, 1886, pp. 269–270; Black to Lucius Fairchild, September 22, 1887, in the Fairchild Papers.

[152]Ross, *Empty Sleeve*, 204–209.

[153]Fairchild to Dear Frank [Mrs. Fairchild], June 13, 1887, in the Fairchild Papers; R.C. Drum to Honorable Governor of _____, June 7, 1887, in Richardson, ed., *Messages and Papers*, 8: 578–579.

[154]*New York Sun*, June 15, 16, 1887; Lankevitch, "G.A.R. in New York State," 214.

[155]Fairchild to Dear Frank, June 19, June 21, 1887, in the Fairchild Papers.

made no official response. President Grover Cleveland immediately rescinded the order, but the damage had already been done.[156] As James "Stumps" Tanner, a two-time New York GAR commander and member of the GAR's pensions committee, pointed out, the president's mistake could be turned into political capital by anti-Cleveland forces. He wrote to Fairchild in August:[157]

> As the years placed themselves between us and the period of the war all were conscious that the *sentiment* of those days was at least dormant if not dead and gone. But one day the President was impelled to interfere with the battle flags. . . and lo and behold there was an upheaval and he saw that in the opinion of the country he had laid impious hands on the Holy of Holies in our Patriotic Temple and he took the back track.
>
> Now, what is the lesson? Certainly this: The man of proven patriotic endeavor and achievement still *has* an advantageous standing before the people at large. We are political fools if we do not take advantage of this patriotic revival.

The stage was thus set for the Bloody Shirt revival that culminated in the presidential election of 1888. Cleveland and the Democrats were placed on the defensive, and the "soldier vote" was viewed as a potentially decisive factor in the campaign.

The Iron Brigade Association's reunion of September, 1887, was a preview of what lay ahead. The reunion took place at the Milwaukee armory building, with the battle flags in attendance. The veterans posed for "soldier photographer" H.H. Bennett of Kilbourn City, sang Army songs, and swapped stories. All seemed normal until Fairchild ally Henry B. Harshaw of Madison introduced a motion to elect association officers by ballot and proposed that John Gibbon not be re-elected president. "It was as if a bomb had suddenly been thrown into the room," noted a

---

[156]L.E. Peterson to Fairchild, June 18, 1887, *ibid.*; E.W. Whitaker to Fairchild, June 18, 1887, *ibid;* An Old Veteran of 7 Years Service and no pension to General Fairchild, June 1887, *ibid.*; Michael Griffin to J.M. Rusk, June 16, 1887, Gov. Mil. Corr.; Dearing, *Veterans in Politics,* 342–344; Ross, *Empty Sleeve,* 208–209; Grover Cleveland to Sec. of War, June 16, 1887, in Richardson, ed., *Messages and Papers,* 8:579.
[157]James Tanner to Lucius Fairchild, August 15, 1887, in the Fairchild Papers.

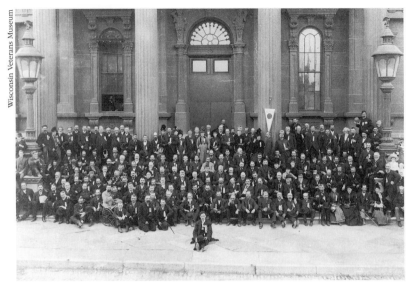

Wisconsin Veterans Museum

The Iron Brigade Association Reunion in Milwaukee in 1887.

reporter.[158] The gathering devolved into "the stormiest meeting the brigade association has ever had. . . ."[159] Amid scenes of "great disorder and confusion," Iron Brigade veterans discussed the Harshaw motion. GAR Adjutant Phil Cheek and Governor Rusk's Quartermaster General, Earl Rogers, led a drive to re-place Gibbon with Lucius Fairchild. Democrats Gil Woodward and Henry Sanford opposed the dump-Gibbon move. The anti-Gibbon forces, of course, were really attempting to unseat Bragg—the senior vice-president—since Gibbon was basically a figurehead. Bragg saw the move for what it was, "an excuse to throw General Bragg overboard."[160]

There was a "hornet's nest in the neighborhood of the little general," reported the *Fond du Lac Commonwealth* as the free-for-all discussion continued.[161] Finally, the veterans cast their votes and Gibbon was re-elected, along with Bragg. The latter, however, chose to step down as senior vice-president, since he did not want to "sow seeds of discord over points of view." W.W. Robinson of Chippewa Falls, a Fairchild ally, thereupon became first vice-president. As Bragg explained to a *Sentinel* reporter, "it is all due to the G.A.R. men, on account of the stand

[158]*Milwaukee Sentinel,* September 14, 15, 1887.
[159]*Ibid.*
[160]*Ibid.*
[161]*Fond du Lac Commonwealth,* September 16, 1887.

I took on the dependent pension bill matter."[162]

President Cleveland's re-election campaign was effectively opposed by Republican veteran organizers. In Wisconsin, both Governor Rusk and ex-Governor Fairchild vigorously campaigned for the election of Benjamin F. Harrison of Indiana, who had been a brigadier general in the war. In the emotional campaign, Cleveland's hiring of a substitute to take his place during the Civil War was endlessly rehashed and condemned, as were his appointments of Confederate officers to federal positions, his supposedly pro-Southern "Cotton Lord" tariff policy, and his veto of the Dependent Pension Bill. Republican veterans barraged Cleveland with Bloody Shirt invective, connecting seemingly unrelated issues—such as the tariff—to Civil War animosities.[163]

A plurality of Wisconsinites and enough other American citizens, particularly those in key states, responded by voting for Harrison. The "soldier vote," and the votes of those men who looked favorably upon the ex-soldiers, was viewed at the time (and since) as providing the Republicans with their narrow margin of victory in the four-candidate race.[164] Not unexpectedly, President Harrison signed a liberal pension bill for Union veterans shortly after taking office. In 1888, the Grand Army of the Republic stood at the pinnacle of its success.

When the GAR held its national encampment in Milwaukee in 1889, politicians watched in awe as nearly 10,000 Wisconsin veterans and numerous detachments from other states paraded sixteen abreast while a quarter of a million citizens cheered them.[165] The most notable absences, however, were the state battle flags. Governor Rusk had retired them before he left

---

[162] *Milwaukee Sentinel,* September 15, 1887.

[163] *Chicago Tribune,* October 3, 4, 1887; Dearing, *Veterans in Politics,* 362–365; Grover Cleveland, Third Annual Message, December 6, 1887, in Richardson, ed., *Messages and Papers,* 8:580–585; James L. Huston, "A Political Response to Industrialism: The Republican Embrace of Protectionist Labor Doctrines," in the *Journal of American History,* 70:35–37 (June, 1983); Logan, *Great Conspiracy,* 658–669; Rusk to G.H. Brintonell, August 2, 1888, Rusk Papers; "Speech at Waupaca, 1888," and John C. Black to Fairchild, September 22, 1887, in the Fairchild Papers; Heck, *Minnesota Veterans,* 150; "Harrison and Cleveland in 1864," in the Rusk Papers.

[164] McMurry, "Soldier Vote in Iowa," 33; *Wisconsin Blue Book, 1983–1984,* p. 686.

[165] *Milwaukee Sentinel,* August 28, 1889.

On the twenty-fifth anniversary of the battle, Governor Rusk and his commissioners at Gettysburg.

office in 1889 to become secretary of agriculture in Harrison's cabinet. When the veterans requested special permission to take a group of Civil War banners to Gettysburg in 1888, on the twenty-fifth anniversary of the battle, he refused, noting the irreplaceable nature of the artifacts. Rusk observed: "I look upon them as being too precious to risk their destruction."[166] Rusk placed the battle flags in the custody of the state historical society "as trustee of the State."[167] Thereafter, society director Reuben G. Thwaites did not permit Wisconsin's Civil War battle flags to appear at public events.

The flags now took up residence in the historical society's rooms in the newly completed south wing of the capitol building.[168] The age of protection and careful preservation had arrived, twenty-three years after the Civil War ended. Repairs had been carried out over the years, but the flags were in delicate condition by the 1880s.[169] The parades, reunions, and exhibits that the flags participated in had obviously contributed to their sorry condition. Indeed, as far as can be determined by present-day examination and from photograhic evidence, it seems likely that veterans and others—anxious to have a memento—had "souvenirized" parts of certain banners by cutting pieces of fab-

[166]J.M. Rusk to L.E. Pond, May 21, 1888, in the Rusk Papers.
[167]R.G. Thwaites to George E. Bryant, January 9, 1903, State Historical Society Administration, General Correspondence, Wisconsin State Archives.
[168]Lord and Ubbelohde, *Clio's Servant*, 74.
[169]Josephine Cleveland to Lucius Fairchild, January 10, 1885, in the Fairchild Papers.

Governor Jeremiah M. Rusk and his one-armed, one-legged staff in September, 1887. Back row, left to right: George W. Baker; F.L. Phillips; Ernst G. Timme, secretary of state; Governor Rusk; Henry B. Harshaw, state treasurer; Charles E. Estabrook, attorney general; J.B. Thayer, superintendent of public instruction; and David Sommers. Middle row: Peter Delmar; Henry Shetter; W.J. Jones; J.W. Curran; W.W. Jones; Benjamin Smith; and Henry P. Fischer. Front row: W.H. McFarland; Mark Smith; and Eugene Bowen.

ric from their delicate folds.

There was, in fact, no longer any need to keep the state battle flags actively deployed. Indeed, their value would be enhanced by preserving them so they could be used for educational and other purposes. Although the battle flags had been retired, they would continue to serve as political and cultural symbols of unique significance.

Reuben Gold Thwaites, for example, supported Senator Pond— Fairchild's Iron Brigade Association ally and now President Harrison's appointee as pension agent at Milwaukee—when he initiated legislation to create a Civil War soldiers' memorial hall to house the state's Civil War artifacts, including the battle flags. Thwaites hoped that the State Historical Society of Wisconsin would become the memorial hall and be authorized to construct a new building near the University of Wisconsin campus. Presciently, he called the capitol "a regular fire trap."[170] In 1895, after an initial failure, state legislators authorized the construction of a "fire-proof structure to protect and accommodate the collections of the State Historical Society of Wisconsin including the state historical museum and the records and relics of the late Civil War."[171] Section four of the act stated: ". . . all property of the State now held in trust by the State Historical Society of Wisconsin and occupying any part of the State Capitol, shall be transferred to said new building. . . . The Governor is hereby authorized. . . to place in said building. . . such battle flags and trophies of the Civil War as are in possession of the State."[172]

The State Historical Society building opened on the University of Wisconsin campus in 1900. The historical society soon clashed with the GAR over control of the battle flag collection. State GAR Commander David G. James of Richland Center, veteran of Shiloh, survivor of Andersonville prison, and soon to be state senator, became critical of the historical society's battle flag display after visiting the new facility. Wandering about "in vain for some time" in search of the flags, James required the assistance of a custodian to locate the display. Then he discovered the flags in a hard-to-reach, overheated room "that served as a light shaft" on the "top story of the building." James informed his old comrades of the "distasteful" situation. The GAR then urged legislators to order the flags back to the capitol.[173] Dutifully, the Legislature passed an "act to provide for a memorial hall at the Capitol" to display war "mementoes" and "relics" while "providing for a return of the battle flags to the Capitol building" in April, 1901.[174]

The proposed memorial hall would not only display artifacts, but also serve as state GAR headquarters. The battle flags would be placed in the rotunda of the capitol in glass cases. "All laws in contravention of this act," directed state lawmakers, "are repealed."[175] Thus, the battle flags had helped endow two museums.

After two years of display in the capitol rotunda, the flags expe-

---

[170]Reuben G. Thwaites to Herbert Baxter Adams, November 8, 1890, State Historical Society, Papers of the Secretary and Librarian; Thwaites to L.E. Pond, July 25, 1890, *ibid.*; Lord and Ubbelohde, *Clio's Servant*, 102; *Soldiers' and Citizens' Album*, 2:398.

[171]*Laws of Wisconsin, 1895,* Chap. 298.

[172]*Ibid.*

[173]Wis. G.A.R., *Proceedings*, 1901, p.63; D.G. James, "The Sixteenth Wisconsin Infantry at Shiloh, Tenn., April 6 and 7, 1862," in F.H. Magdenburg, comp., *Wisconsin at Shiloh: Report of the Commission* (Milwaukee, 1909), 33–45.

[174]*Laws of Wisconsin, 1901,* Chap. 125.

[175]*Ibid.*, also see *SHSW Proceedings* (1903), 36; Lord and Ubbelohde, *Clio's Servant,* 141.

rienced another change of environment. On the evening of February 27, 1904, calamity struck the state capitol. A malfunctioning gas jet in the second-story cloakroom kindled a fire. Faulty water mains, injuries to Madison's fire chief, and other confusions prevented early quenching of the blaze. Thereafter, the fire could not be extinguished. Governor La Follette and 200 University students carried books and papers out of the flaming building. Next day, little remained of the "splendid building but the great dome and the ruined walls," reported the *Wisconsin State Journal.*[176] The GAR Memorial Hall was completely gutted. But miraculously, the flags survived.

While fire raged, Jacob Barr, a traveling salesman from Chicago, and Elmore Elver, a Madison hotel proprietor, had rushed into the flame-engulfed capitol. They broke open the flag cases in the rotunda and carried "the sacred relics" to the safety of nearby snowbanks.[177] The flags traveled back to the historical society for safekeeping. Thwaites explained to a friend: "You, of course, by this time have heard all about our great fire at the Capitol. Everything is gone except the north wing. . . . The battle flags of the G.A.R. are now in our keeping here, where they will remain for many years more. . . . It is a very great change for our little town and there is consternation everywhere."[178]

Wisconsin's battle flags remained at the historical society for a decade while designers, architects, masons, and laborers built a new and larger state capitol.[179] By 1914, much of the work had been completed. In June, the aging Boys in Blue of the Grand Army of the Republic held their annual encampment in the Assembly Chamber, and Governor Francis E. McGovern ordered the battle flags back to the capitol for the occasion. Thwaites willingly complied, having spent the preceding ten years reingratiating himself and the historical society with the GAR through the medium of the Wisconsin History Commis-

[176]*Wisconsin State Journal,* February 27, 1904; George E. Bryant, *The Capitol Fire* (Madison, 1904).
[177]*Wisconsin State Journal,* February 27, 1904.
[178]Reuben G. Thwaites to F.J. Turner, February 29, 1904, in the Thwaites Papers, Wisconsin State Archives.
[179]*SHSW Proceedings* (1914), 46; Lord and Ubbelohde, *Clio's Servant,* 206; Bryant, *The Capitol Fire;* George E. Bryant, *Classic and Beautiful Our Proposed Capitol* (Madison, 1905).

The Wisconsin GAR Encampment of 1914 in the assembly chambers of the state capitol. The battle flags can be seen furled in the rear and to the left.

sion. Charles E. Estabrook, a GAR activist, headed the commission, which published memoirs of various ex-soldiers, as well as statistical and documentary works on Civil War-related topics.[180]

The elderly veterans appreciated Governor McGovern's gesture of kindness "best of all." The old ex-soldiers stood guard beside the gauze-covered flags, which were posted along the east wall of the Assembly Chamber. "No patriotic address during our encampment could equal in eloquence the silent presence of those old war-time banners of ours—worn and faded, torn and bullet-riddled, yet beautiful," wrote Jerome Watrous.[181] After the meeting, the battle flags were deposited in the governor's vault while work continued on the north wing of the capitol, where the new GAR memorial hall would be located.[182]

Workers completed decorating the GAR Memorial Hall in March,

[180] *SHSW Proceedings* (1914), 46; Lord and Ubbelohde, *Clio's Servant*, 142–143; Wis. G.A.R., *Proceedings,* 1914, pp. 127–128; H.W. Rood, *A Little Flag Book* (n.p., 1919), 38.

[181] Wis. G.A.R., *Proceedings,* 1914, pp. 127–128.

[182] Lord and Ubbelohde, *Clio's Servant*, 504; Rood, *Little Flag Book,* 38; Rood, *Memorial Day Annual, 1916* (Madison, 1916), 20; *Laws of Wisconsin, 1909,* Chap. 47.

1917. Architect Lew Porter designed the hall for the GAR with its elaborate vaulted ceilings and frescoes naming the battles in which Wisconsin units had participated. Hosea W. Rood of Milton, a veteran of the Twelfth Wisconsin, schoolteacher, and state GAR patriotic instructor, became custodian of the facility, and he arranged the museum displays. Large glass-fronted cases were built to house the battle flag collection, and in December the flags were brought up from the governor's vault.[183] On Flag Day—June 14, 1918—the GAR Memorial Hall was dedicated.[184]

Iron Brigade veteran Jerome Watrous presented a dedication speech entitled, "Looking Over Our Old Battle Flags." He reviewed the major developments which had occurred in the United States since 1865. Involvement in the Spanish-American War and now in the Great War in Europe, he explained, had underscored the importance of national unity achieved by the veterans of his generation. New generations had grown up since the Civil War, while tens of thousands of newly arrived immigrants had become citizens. What, asked Watrous, would remind these men and women of the supreme test of the Union and its staggering costs? As the old men of the GAR passed away, how would the boys of 1861–1865 be remembered? It was the battle flags that would remain immortal: "Those. . . old, faded, torn emblems of our great, strong nation." The flags had come to represent the Civil War veterans' very experience. As Watrous concluded: "We had been woven into the colors."[185]

[183]Hosea W. Rood, January 10, March 17, April 20, 1917, in Rood Diary, 1917, Archives, Wisconsin Veterans Museum.

[184]Rood to G.A.R. Patriotic Instructors, May 21, 1918, in the Rood papers, Wisconsin Veterans Museum.

[185]J.A. Watrous, "Looking Over Our Old Battle Flags," and J.A. Watrous, "Program for the Dedication of Grand Army Memorial Hall in the Capitol, Madison, Wisconsin, June 14, 1918," both in Archives, Wisconsin Veterans Museum; Wis. G.A.R., *Proceedings,* 1919, p. 71.

Epilogue

The Wisconsin Civil War battle flags remained undisturbed in their glass cases on the fourth floor of the state capitol for nearly fifty years. The GAR Memorial Hall Museum, meanwhile, passed into the control of the newly created Wisconsin Department of Veterans Affairs in 1945. In 1964, museum curators from the State Historical Society of Wisconsin catalogued the battle flag collection during a general upgrading of the museum displays.[186]

Thirteen years later, in 1977, a Smithsonian Institution consultant visited the GAR Museum to examine the battle flag collection, that by then was sadly in need of conservation.[187] Subsequent conservation grant proposals to the National Endowment for the Arts failed, but in 1981 private donations from a wide range of individuals, school children, corporations, veterans' groups, and foundations as well as legislatively approved funds from the Veterans Trust Fund initiated the Wisconsin Civil War Battle Flag Conservation Project.[188] The project is an ongoing one and to date has conserved 110 historic flags, including those of the Iron Brigade. When the GAR Museum moved from the state capitol to adjacent modern facilities being developed for the Wisconsin Department of Veterans Affairs, the battle flags moved too. Portions of the conserved flag collection are displayed at the new Wisconsin Veterans Museum, which was opened in 1993. There, the public may view the proud remnants of banners designed, created, and borne in battle during the time of Abraham Lincoln.

---

[186] *Wisconsin Statutes*, Chap. 45, Veterans Affairs, Benefits and Memorials, 45.01, G.A.R. Memorial Hall, and 45.02, Memorial Collection; John R. Moses to Joe Nusbaum, September 30, 1962; Leslie H. Fishel, Jr., to John R. Moses, June 30, 1964; Proposed Plan for Restoration of the G.A.R. Memorial Hall, all in Wisconsin Veterans Museum Records; and Paul Vanderbilt, "A Museum Transformed: Grand Army Memorial Hall in Madison," in *WMH*, 48:295–296 (Summer, 1965).

[187] Dennis K. McDaniel to Grace Rogers Cooper, May 31, 1977, Wisconsin Veterans Museum Records.

[188] Grant applications to the National Endowment for the Arts, June 14, 1978, and June 1, 1979; Minutes of the Regular Meeting of the Joint Committee on Finance Under S.13.101, June 18, 1980, and Transfers and Supplements, June 26, 1980; Richard Zeitlin to John R. Moses, January 18, 1982, all in the Wisconsin Veterans Museum Records; and Howard M. Madaus, "Rally 'Round the Flag, Boys," in *Lore*, 32:3–13 (Spring, 1982).